THE TURNAROUND PRESCRIPTION

THE
TURNAROUND PRESCRIPTION

REPOSITIONING TROUBLED COMPANIES

MARK R. GOLDSTON

THE FREE PRESS
A Division of Macmillan, Inc.
New York

Maxwell Macmillan Canada
Toronto

Maxwell Macmillan International
New York   Oxford   Singapore   Sydney

The Free Press
A Division of Macmillan, Inc.
866 Third Avenue, New York, N.Y. 10022

Maxwell Macmillan Canada, Inc.
1200 Eglinton Avenue East
Suite 200
Don Mills, Ontario M3C 3N1

Macmillan, Inc. is part of the Maxwell Communication Group of Companies.

Printed in the United States of America

printing number

1 2 3 4 5 6 7 8 9 10

Library of Congress Cataloging-in-Publication Data

Goldston, Mark R.
    The turnaround prescription: repositioning troubled companies/
Mark R. Goldston.
        p.   cm.
    Includes index.
    ISBN 0–02–912395–X
    1. Corporate turnarounds.   I. Title.
HD58.8.G63   1992
658.4'063—dc20   92–10752
                                                            CIP

To my mom Rosalind, who always had faith in me and convinced me to commit these thoughts to text.

To my incredible wife NancyJane, whose never ending support, love, input, and commitment were a constant source of strength in helping me to complete this book and become the person that I am.

To Adam and Ryan, the two best sons a father could ever have, for the love and spirit they provided and for being a constant source of joy in my life.

And lastly, to my departed dad, who taught me more about life and business than he ever could have imagined and who, regretfully, never lived to see the fruits of those efforts.

CONTENTS

PREFACE

After spending eight years compiling the strategies and techniques detailed in this book and over three years actually writing, I am presenting what I believe to be a practical, "how to" handbook for executives involved in conducting the turnaround of a troubled business. In that sense, *The Turnaround Prescription* is an extension of my professional being.

The term "turnaround" has been used in a number of different contexts, for example, by individuals who have helped to take a business and increase its sales and profits. While that can absolutely be characterized as stellar performance and the practitioners are to be admired for their efforts, such situations do not truly merit the designation "turnaround."

In this book, I will consider businesses whose sales and profits have fallen off precipitously, and who are considered to be less of a factor in their primary business than they were five years ago to be true turnaround candidates. Companies that have been troubled since day one, and never really achieved a level that could be termed successful, are not true turnaround candidates.

Subsegments of the term turnaround refer to the specific discipline on which each is based: the "marketing turnaround," the "financial turnaround," the "operations turnaround," which are performed by the vice-presidents, senior vice-presidents, or other executives of the respective disciplines. In these situations, that particular aspect of the firm may have "fallen from grace," thus holding back the entity from realizing its full potential.

The phrase "marketing turnaround" comes from my experience in completing this task for the first time in 1984. Marketing turnarounds became my calling card as I gave more than seventy-five speeches during the 1984–1991 period and I actively pursued career opportunities requiring someone to spearhead the effort to perform such a turnaround on a consumer product business.

My first foray into the field of marketing turnarounds was at the cosmetic giant Revlon, Inc. In 1984, we helped to engineer the turnaround of the mass-market fragrance business from a significant loss to a respectable profit, while also effecting a 33 percent increase in market share.

After Revlon I headed to Fabergé, then a tired marketer of consumer products in the toiletries and fragrance industries, which had truly taken a huge tumble from its high-flying status in the 1970s featuring Joe Namath for Brut, Margaux Hemingway for Babe, and Lola Falana for Tigress. Fabergé had become a low-priced player in the toiletries business competing solely on the basis of price.

I joined Fabergé as executive vice-president of marketing in 1986 and became president in 1987. There my staff and I helped to effect a true marketing turnaround in an eighteen-month period. Sales increased almost 25 percent and profits soared over 50 percent, making Fabergé once again a formidable, creative marketer that was well respected within the industry. Late in 1987, Fabergé acquired Elizabeth Arden, turning the firm into a $1 billion beauty products powerhouse that was sold to Unilever, N.V. in 1988 for approximately $1.6 billion.

In 1988 I joined Reebok International Ltd. as the chief marketing officer of a firm that had gone from zero to one billion dollars faster than virtually any firm in history. In the midst of a terrible identity crisis the firm's stock had dropped from $24 to approximately $9 a share by August of 1988. The image shoes that had carried Reebok to glory were considered tired by the fickle sneaker consumers, who ordained Nike as the performance brand of choice and were gravitating towards upstart L.A. Gear and resuscitated Keds as the image brands of choice.

At Reebok, the team I headed created a controversial, aggressive strategy designed to make Reebok both a fashion and a performance company, without sacrificing the dynamic imagery on which the firm was based. We developed distinct units for Lifestyle and Performance and set different marketing strategies and support programs for each unit.

During my Reebok tenure we created perhaps the most innovative and successful sneaker of all time: The Reebok Pump, a $170 inflatable basketball shoe that spawned an entire line of "Pump" products across several different product categories. During 1990–1991, the Pump generated approximately $500 million in sales. If the Pump were a stand-alone company, it would have been the fourth largest sneaker company in the United States, behind Nike, Reebok, and L.A. Gear.

Further, we marketed a whole host of other innovations including the Reebok Visible Energy Return System, the Hexalite Cushioning System, the Energaire System, and the

Agility System for children, just to name a few. In all, the innovations introduced during my tenure at Reebok accounted for roughly $750 million in sales in 1991 and helped to make the company into an image *and* performance powerhouse catering both to performance enthusiasts and fashion seekers, who want to wear the latest styles.

After leaving Reebok, I joined Odyssey Partners, L.P., the prestigious New York based leveraged buyout/investment firm founded in 1978 by Jack Nash and Leon Levy, two absolutely brilliant former top officers at Oppenheimer & Company. Odyssey Partners has majority ownership positions in approximately twenty different companies, with a net asset value in the several billion dollar range. In addition, the firm manages roughly $1 billion in capital invested by a select group of limited partners. Odyssey Partners is one of the most extraordinary organizations of its kind in the world staffed with some of the brightest individuals I have ever been together with under one roof.

Odyssey assembled an internal operating unit of ex-presidents of companies with diverse backgrounds to form a "turnaround team" that would supervise the management of Odyssey's undervalued portfolio companies and assist in the search, evaluation, and acquisition of new companies. Collectively, we helped manage roughly ten different companies.

Our diverse backgrounds and specialties in marketing, sales, finance, operations/production, and the like taught us more about the art of turnarounds than any single corporate experience could have provided. If I could take that team into virtually any corporate disaster imaginable, I would bet my last nickel that within twelve to twenty-four months the entity would be significantly better off than it was when we started.

The turnaround team, with the input and guidance of two of the general partners, Brian Young and Steve Friedman, the visionaries who assembled the team, made major strides in such

firms as Revell/Monogram Models, Eagle Food Centers, Forst-
mann Wool, Cole of California, Catalina Swimwear, Colonial
Corporation of America, and Black Box Corporation during the
1989–1991 period.

In October 1991, I went off in pursuit of another turnaround
candidate, accepting the position as president and chief operating
officer of L.A. Gear, Inc., the troubled athletic footwear and
apparel manufacturer.

Based in Los Angeles, California, L.A. Gear was the na-
tion's third-ranked athletic footwear company in 1991, having
reached a total worldwide revenue level of over $600 million.
After a fabulously successful run between 1987 and 1990 as one
of the fastest growing companies in the world and one of the
hottest stocks on Wall Street, L.A. Gear encountered some rather
serious problems relating to over-inventorization, lack of focus
in its brand image and marketing efforts, some unsuccessful
high-priced endorsement deals, and a host of other problems that
may beset a high-flying, entrepreneurial company as it races
towards the billion dollar sales level in less than five years.

During 1991, L.A. Gear reported pretax profit losses in
excess of $67 million, making it ripe for a total turnaround in its
operational and marketing efforts. Clearly the situation represents a major challenge that appears to be tailor-made for many
of the theories espoused in *The Turnaround Prescription*.

With that as a backdrop, I decided to write *The Turnaround
Prescription* because I believe that these principles are basic in
nature, combining some elements of skill with a lot of common
sense, and that they can help middle and senior corporate managers guide their firms out of troubled waters. It is my distinct
hope that after reading this book, you will feel that it is an
invaluable weapon in your arsenal and that it helps you to understand the importance of a methodological system for creating
the strategic vision and operating plan required to effect a corporate turnaround.

INTRODUCTION

In 1983, while working as the senior director of marketing for the Fragrance Division of Revlon, Inc., I was compelled to create a framework that could be used by senior executives to resuscitate the marketing efforts and imagery of fallen brands and corporate nameplates. Revlon, gravely in need of a complete marketing turnaround, hired me to create a blueprint for performing the task successfully within the Fragrance Division of the U.S. unit.

Trained in marketing at the revered consumer product institutions of Johnson & Johnson, Bristol-Myer's/Clairol, and Chesebrough-Pond's, my perspective on the problem was largely confined to how to create increased consumer demand and restored imagery, while at the same time helping to generate enough internal cost savings to fuel new marketing efforts. I was drawn to the concept of utilizing the existing manufacturing facilities of the company to help create new products, given the reluctance of senior management to invest in long-range tooling for indeterminate marketing projects.

This fascination with alternative uses for the existing plant and equipment resource base, coupled with a stepwise analytical approach to the marketing task, led me to uncover a methodology that worked successfully in a number of situations. The phrase I chose to describe the process was ''the marketing turnaround,'' and I began to call the framework of the process ''engineering a marketing turnaround.''

Armed with the marketing turnaround blueprint, I began giving speeches to various business organizations and academic institutions and became a regular featured speaker at Northwestern University's J. L. Kellogg School of Management Executive Education Seminars on Consumer Marketing Strategy. As the lone business executive in a one-week program dominated by the stellar marketing faculty of one of the world's top-ranked business schools, I felt compelled to create a format for the marketing turnaround blueprint that was easy to understand and clearly focused on explaining the procedure and delivering results.

I have been giving the ''marketing turnaround'' seminars at the Kellogg School executive program since 1984 to diverse groups of sixty to a hundred executives. Throughout this period, an overwhelming number of participants have told me that they felt this was the first format for conducting a marketing-based turnaround that appeared to be applicable to a whole range of consumer and industrial businesses. Both the faculty of the Kellogg School and the executive participants in the program urged me to set this blueprint down in written form and publish it so that others could benefit from its theories and procedures. A host of problems far broader in scope than those contained within the marketing function alone have necessitated the expansion of the turnaround blueprint to the entire spectrum of a business enterprise, including finance, operations, R&D, sales, and so on.

The Turnaround Prescription features eleven symptoms of a firm in trouble and ten surefire "prescriptions" to help address and solve the symptomatic problems. Because the scope of the problems outlined in the eleven symptoms and ten prescriptions goes far beyond the area of marketing alone, they constitute Part I of this book, "Engineering a Corporate Turnaround." Part II of the book, entitled "Engineering a Marketing Turnaround: Concepts and Cases," outlines a detailed step-by-step procedure for analyzing a firm that is a marketing turnaround candidate and explains the process by which it can be turned around within twelve to twenty-four months. The book contains several original theories regarding the turnaround process including:

- *Trademark Leveraging*—how to take existing or dormant brand names or trademarks and position them to generate incremental volume for a firm.

- *The Corporate Capabilities Matrix*—a device that helps to highlight the alternative uses of existing manufacturing facilities and tooling banks for purposes of creating increased operating efficiencies and a substantially reduced new product development cycle time line.

- *The New Product Marketing Decision Tree*—a fifteen-step process designed to lead the firm from the conceptualization/target identification phase all the way through to introduction of the product.

- *The Business Building Octagon*—an eight-step procedure to be used by senior management in assessing the proper progression for a firm to take in pursuit of bringing a product to market and successfully "pushing" it into the retailer and "pulling" it through to the consumer. The Business Building Octagon is more of a senior level macro-view, whereas the Marketing Decision Tree is more of a middle-management micro-view process.

- *The Concept of "Value Engineering"*—explains how a firm can evaluate its products and manufacturing procedures to create serious cost savings without diminishing the quality or performance of the products/organizations. These savings can often be used as the source of a business-building "war chest" to help an entity that is cash starved and cannot generate incremental spending dollars.

- *The Corporate Life Cycle Analysis*—a tool created from the famous product life cycle analysis taught in academic institutions. It turns the company itself into a product and analyzes where each of its products lies in the various phases of the life cycle from introduction to growth, maturity, and decline. The analysis suggests the correct balance to be struck between these phases and provides a unique opportunity to take a "snapshot" of a business entity at a point in time and determine where it is heading.

- *Product Positioning: Marketing Birth Certificate*—explains the intricacies involved in correctly positioning a product as it enters the marketplace. Further, it describes how most new products fail due to improper positioning which results from an inadequate segmentation analysis of the market category to be entered.

- *Conducting an Effective Segmentation Analysis*—describes the methodology that must be used in order to conduct a meaningful segmentation analysis and suggests variables to be used as a means of determining where market gaps exist.

- *The Mission Statement*—describes how to create an effective mission statement for a brand or company and how to use that device as the guiding light for developing various micro-strategies for running an effective business.

- *The Line Positioning Matrix*—a device enabling management to review all of the products or line-extensions within an entity and ferret out those that are positioned to cannibalize existing brands within the company's portfolio.

This book should serve as a handbook for middle- and senior-level executives—a "playbook" for executing a total operational turnaround, or a marketing turnaround within one or two years. It contains practical theories and procedures that I have applied with a high degree of success at some of the largest companies in the United States between 1983 and 1992.

I believe the reader will view this book as an invaluable tool for uncovering the specific problems that may be crippling a business entity, as well as the "turnaround blueprint" for actually solving those problems and restoring the entity to a position of growth, profitability, and respect within its marketplace.

The Turnaround Prescription is divided into individual segments, so that the busy executive or academic can either read the book cover to cover, or select the specific sections that may pertain to an immediate problem. This single book, containing all of the requisite elements for a corporate or marketing turnaround, is something no executive should be without in the uncertain decade of the 1990s.

PART I

ENGINEERING A CORPORATE TURNAROUND

1

TURNAROUND DIAGNOSTICS

When a company is in "trouble" and in need of a turnaround, the whole world seems to know it and the entity becomes something of a spectacle for the business community to feed upon. The true art of management is in reading the symptoms of a company heading for trouble and taking the appropriate steps to fend off disaster.

Turnaround management has become a buzzword of the 1990s, given the incredible number of businesses that were over-leveraged in the 1980s and have run into trouble attempting to service steady or increasing debt service payments in the face of flat or declining sales trends. In some instances, the businesses themselves are relatively healthy in the absolute, but the inordinate levels of debt were predicated on unrealistic growth trends that never materialized. The turnaround process can be very different for these companies than it is for the truly troubled business, which is fighting a combination of problems. High interest payments, declining revenues, increasing costs due to manufacturing and or manpower inefficiencies, and a product line or technological capacity that is rapidly becoming obsolete are all problems that affect firms.

Whether the turnaround must address the troubled core entity or merely an overleveraged asset, the signs of trouble can usually be camouflaged to those executives locked in the ivory towers. A diagnostic tool and a format for solving the various problems within these businesses can be the most valuable asset any company owns.

Many times a marketing turnaround can be conducted, completely fixing the business problem. In other instances, an overall diagnosis of the health of the business must be conducted before a determination can be made as to whether the firm is in need of a more encompassing turnaround plan.

Assessing the state of a consumer product, leisure company, service organization, or retailer from a consumer standpoint can fail to uncover the underlying symptoms that have caused the problem to develop. Businesses do not decline on their own; they are managed into and through the process. Although the decline of the product line itself may signal the need for remedial action, many times it is personnel, manufacturing, financial, or marketing problems that have a negative impact on the business. Therefore, before conducting a marketing turnaround, the business team charged with engineering that feat must determine whether the symptoms require a total turnaround. If so, the following turnaround prescriptions will most certainly be an invaluable tool to the management team.

The "Turnaround Diagnostics" presented here consist of eleven telltale symptoms followed by ten surefire prescriptions.

While very few businesses will have all eleven symptoms—and ones that do may well be terminal cases—many symptoms go unnoticed because they appear to be unspectacular when viewed individually. This is the business equivalent of the silent killer. Because many of these business dysfunctions are interrelated, together they paint a picture of a troubled asset (company) in dire need of remedial attention.

The turnaround prescriptions described in this section of the book are presented in a sequential format, which should serve as a blueprint to guide managers through the turnaround process and help them to determine where they are in that process and how to observe the proverbial "light at the end of the tunnel" (making sure that it is not a train coming the other way). Clearly, the turnaround diagnostics outlined in this book extend far beyond the marketing function alone, and deal with the difficult process of trying to coordinate several seemingly disparate malfunctions at the same time.

2

SYMPTOMS OF A FIRM IN NEED OF A TURNAROUND

SYMPTOM 1: *The firm is losing money from an operating profit standpoint.*

While this would seem to be an obvious sign of a firm in need of a turnaround, it would amaze most people to know that loss of operating profit is commonly attributed to the "victim phenomenon" within many troubled companies. Specifically, the companies that typically suffer from a precipitous drop in operating profit on a quarterly or annual basis reason that they (the company) are victims of uncontrollable circumstances which can range from unseasonable weather to a tough economy, declining market, or retailer de-inventorization. Rarely does the senior management team of a company that exhibits a declining operating profit trend practice introspection; rather they delude themselves into believing the circumstantial explanation, which over time becomes a self-fulfilling prophecy.

It is critical to the success of any turnaround endeavor that the management team vested with the responsibility for developing and/or executing the overall plan assess the situation realistically and remove personal feelings from the equation. Obviously this is easier said than done, but it is absolutely essential for the proper execution of the turnaround prescription, which often involves making several very tough business and/or personnel decisions.

SYMPTOM 2: *Market share has declined steadily or precipitously over a twelve- to twenty-four-month period.*

The concept of a company or product line exhibiting one or two years of steadily declining market share sounds like a situation that would lead senior management to realize that the business is in trouble and in need of a turnaround. But often that is not the case. The affected firm may utilize many of the same "victim" excuses when describing a declining market share situation as they will when describing the erosion of their operating profit. In most cases, the declining share is deemed to be circumstantial or the result of adverse market dynamics, competitive introductions, or declining overall demand for the product category. Again, as with Symptom 1, this can easily become a self-fulfilling prophecy that is welcomed by members of the organization who should ordinarily be held accountable for the subpar performance.

When a product line or company market share is allowed to decline unchecked over a twelve- to twenty-four-month period, by definition the entity is facing a shrinking core and the inherent cost of doing business as usual becomes excessively high. In cases where the overhead structure of the entity is predicated on the unit volume production level and the volume drops below that level for an extended period, the entity will experience a situation known as negative manufacturing variance. The manpower, machinery, and administrative expenses of a business entity are normally allocated over a universe of widgets, which in totality delivers an acceptable cost per widget. In laymen's terms, then, negative manufacturing variance means that those same expenses must now be allocated to a smaller widget universe, so that the cost factor per widget goes up significantly, and the overall profitability of the entity may be threatened.

One of the major risks of the "denial reaction" within management ranks is that the necessary overhead reduction measures, which must be taken in response to something that is more than a temporary or instantaneous volume decline, do not get employed and the entity falls farther into the negative profitability mode.

In a closely monitored company with superior understanding of its internal expense structure and a highly sensitive management team, when the level of the profit base in response to volume declines, initial steps can be taken to provide for a more flexible overhead structure that is less encumbering and more responsive to a volatile unit volume base.

SYMPTOM 3: *Quality managers are departing from the firm with a degree of regularity.*

Human capital is perhaps the single most valuable asset any company has, but all too often it is the most neglected, worst maintained asset of all. Without fail, one can spot the companies that are in trouble financially and in need of a turnaround by observing a high degree of defections within the middle and senior management ranks:

The high managerial turnover levels are usually the result of a number of factors, including:

- The "guilt" factor, where managers believe they were instrumental in causing the problems and feel the need to extract themselves from the situation.

- The "blame" factor, where managers fear that they will be blamed for the problems of the business—either rightly or wrongly—and do not want to wait around for what they perceive as their imminent termination from the company.

- The "frustration" factor, which causes managers in a tough business situation to feel that there is no successful solution to the firm's problems and that they can no longer make a productive contribution.

• The "neglect" factor, in whch the manager believes that
  the firm no longer cares about things such as succession
  planning, career growth, cross-functional training, and the
  like.

Therefore, it is critical in companies that are losing key employees at a high rate for top managers to quickly recognize that one
or all of these dynamics may be at work within the organization
and that the exodus may be the precursor to a much more severe
problem, which will affect the continuity of execution.

Thus far we have described three symptoms of a company in
need of turnaround: decline in operating profit, steady or precipitous decline in market share over a twelve- to twenty-four-
month period, and the exodus of more than one or two managers
from the organization over a relatively short (three- to six-month)
period. Clearly, when these three symptoms are present, Symptom 4 will logically appear next.

SYMPTOM 4: *Company pride is greatly diminished and individual initiative seems to be at lower levels, resulting in problems relating to idea generation and information flow.*

A reduction in company pride and initiative is likely to be the immediate result of a decline in profitability and market share and a relatively high degree of managerial exodus. And when pride and initiative decline, the flow of ideas will be reduced, resulting in a general decomposition of the firm's information flow structure. Morale is a powerful component in the effective operation of any company, and the tangible results of the firm play a major role in how the employees feel about themselves and their employer.

Imagine a situation where the base business is declining and the need for new ideas and interdepartmental communication is more important than ever before, but the work force is demoralized by the poor performance of the business and the seeming insensitivity of the senior management team. This set of conditions indicates that things are bad and are going to get worse. And when the general work force and outsiders become aware that the firm is in need of a turnaround before the senior management team acknowledges that fact, company morale and idea flow decline exponentially and potentially could throw a troubled firm into a crisis mode.

SYMPTOM 5: *The company facilities appear to be run down. Overall cleanliness and quality standards seem greatly diminished and manufacturing equipment is only repaired after breakdown.*

There is perhaps no more valuable asset to a manufacturing organization than its physical plant and machinery, and the state of readiness and overall condition of the facilities is usually in direct relation to the most recent twelve- to twenty-four-month revenue and profit trend. A manufacturing company in decline will often try to milk the entity in the short term to avoid making value improvements in the near term. In many cases, the manufacturing equipment of an organization becomes a virtual "chop shop," where unused machines are dismantled to provide spare parts for other machines on the production floor. In doing so, the company is, by definition, reducing both its capacity base and its overall asset value.

Successful companies in the manufacturing sector are typified by rigid quality control standards that border on fanaticism. Clearly the quality, appearance, functionality, fit, and finish of a company's products make a very strong statement to the retail and consumer public. Any precipitous drop-off in any of these variables sends a strong signal to the target audience that the firm and/or the products have declined from their previous position of strength. Further, the overall attitude of the work force has a direct impact on the quality of work performed on the manufacturing floor, and a combination of Symptoms 3 and 4 can lead to a significant reduction in quality of the products produced.

SYMPTOM 6: *The company is having a hard time generating cash or is eating it.*

This is often a futile situation, because the company is not operated on a cash flow basis. The senior divisional managers of many large corporations have never been held accountable for cash flow delivery, but instead have been evaluated on contribution, gross profit delivery, or revenue goals.

Managing a business for cash is a learned practice, which often times involves reprioritizing projects, altering inventory and in-stock positions, making purchasing arrangements with suppliers, practicing value engineering of existing products and facilities, and modification of processes.

When faced with a cash crisis, most managers employ "the big drawer" theory: They throw invoices to be paid into a large receptacle and wait for the creditor to inquire several times about payment before the invoice is paid. The sophisticated terminology for this phenomenon is "management of float." When the money cannot come in fast enough to keep the payments on schedule, the conditions explained in Symptom 5 come to the surface.

A major source of cash can be tapped within the new receivables base of the company, but in instances where the cash position is suspect, the firm must go out and secure additional money through debt financing. Unfortunately, banks do not typically loan money to companies or individuals who are strapped for cash, so they require collateral to protect them in the event of default. The most obvious and fertile collateral of a cash-starved company is its new receivables base. Therefore, although new money is flowing in from the accounts receivable, the proceeds are already spoken for and are therefore virtually frozen within the company's balance sheet.

SYMPTOM 7: *On-hand inventory levels exceed the normal three- to four-month supply level and more importantly do not accurately reflect the mix of the product line at retail.*

This symptom is generally most likely to be found in consumer goods manufacturing companies and it can be a debilitating factor in the successful operation of any company. When a company has multiple products or stockkeeping units (SKUs), it is imperative that they accurately read the rate of sale at the retail level and continually update and modify their production schedules to balance their inventory weighting with the retail rate of consumption. Unfortunately, when this does not happen, companies find themselves in an elevated inventory position, with goods that are out of mix with the retail rate of sale.

The mix problems of manufacturing companies create obsolete products, which ultimately lead to costly write-downs and then write-offs. The problem is further compounded when a firm is overinventoried and it does not have available space, funds, or facilities to manufacture the timely products. It is then forced to try and dispose of the on-hand, less desirable inventory.

This leads to an entirely new set of problems relating to the ''dumping'' or closing out of merchandise in the marketplace, which ties up retailers' open-to-buy funds and, more critically, offers consumers less expensive products that they can purchase in place of full-price current products.

Yet another major problem for overinventoried, out-of-mix companies involves the availability to them of leveraged capital to fund the ongoing needs of the business. Several companies have what is known as a "revolver," or revolving line of credit, which is typically secured by the finished goods inventory of the company. On average, the banks will loan companies forty cents on the dollar of inventory. However, when a firm is saddled with out-of-date, obsolete goods, which are about to be offered at reduced or closeout prices, the funds they can draw upon are severely reduced because the forty cents is applied to a smaller dollar value.

It is imperative that senior managers in companies experiencing this inventory imbalance do not delude themselves into believing the convenient explanation—that the market is undergoing a temporary aberrant trend and that it will right itself shortly, thus restoring the current inventory supply to mix. The market aberration theory is a common way to avoid the real cause of share decline and misguided forecasting that many companies choose to believe rather than face reality. Unfortunately, this theory is just one more example of the executive denial reaction typically associated with declining companies and serves further to exacerbate the situation by delaying the proper response to the real market trend.

If one were to review the seven symptoms just presented and notice the interrelation between them, the picture of a firm in need of a turnaround starts to become very clear. Further, it is not uncommon for these symptoms to work in concert with one another. In fact, the number of companies in need of turnaround management assistance is far greater than most managers realize, especially since managers often try to rationalize many of these symptoms as temporary aberrations.

Against this backdrop, the next four symptoms in the analysis will help to complete the picture of the classic case involving a company (especially one that manufactures and sells products to the consumer) that is in need of a turnaround.

SYMPTOM 8: *Expense reductions have resulted in a marked decrease in research and development, new product development, and advertising and promotional spending.*

Symptom 8 is perhaps best labeled as the "eighties disease" or the "sign of the LBO." Many firms during this highly leveraged decade were forced to make drastic reductions in overall spending to meet an inordinately high level of interest expense effected by the leveraged acquisition of the company.

Alternatively, companies that found themselves in markets that were either shrinking, becoming more competitive, or finding the technological uniqueness of their products to be diminished were forced to make their profit projections in the face of flat to declining revenue trends.

This phenomenon was (and is) especially prevalent in publicly traded companies, who became infected with "quarter-itis," a disease that causes management to mortgage the future of the business for the sake of meeting quarterly profit objectives which may have been unrealistic. These firms and their managers must one day pay the piper for those deeds, which typically result in the business declining or being forced into an obsolete mode.

The shortsighted approach to managing business, a charge often leveled at American management by the Japanese, can negatively transform a very powerful entity for the sake of achieving near-term profit objectives. In retrospect, many of the executives who guided firms into those situations have said that if they had it to do over again (and could be assured of job security through the turmoil), they would not have cut back on R&D, new product development, or advertising and promotion, because in effect such cutbacks deprived the existing business of vital fuel (advertising and promotion), while cutting off a future revenue stream to the company as the result of a new technology (R&D), which would ultimately result in the introduction of a new product.

Among the first things firms and individuals look for when reviewing the financial statements of companies under consideration for acquisition are the R&D, new products, and advertising and promotion lines of the profit-and-loss statement, because many times this will help to explain the firm's current profitability and, more importantly, it provides a realistic assessment of the timing and potential for future volume and profit growth. The savvy investor can easily uncover a firm that has been "dressed up" for sale or has succumbed to the "slash and burn" techniques associated with cutting the items described in Symptom 8.

This actually extends far beyond the rather small acquisition community of corporations and buyout firms. The individual and institutional investors who purchase stocks and bonds of publicly traded companies often closely peruse the reported financial statements of particular companies (annual report, 10-K, 10-Q, 8-K, etc.) and pay close attention to recent expense reduction trends.

These individuals and analysts will view a significant cutback in R&D, new product development, or advertising and promotion as a sign that the firm has been experiencing financial problems and that the future growth potential of that company (in spite of its healthy looking current financial reports) may be suspect. More often than not, publicly traded stocks are purchased for the long term and therefore the focus is not so much on the recent past and current condition of the company as it is on the firm's capital base and future growth potential.

SYMPTOM 9: *In the case of a consumer product, the item is no longer the "brand of choice"—it may be part of a consumer's purchase wardrobe, but usage may be sharply reduced from previous levels.*

Often, this ninth symptom is not recognized by companies until too late, and the brand has already experienced serious franchise erosion. Typically, consumers will purchase more than one brand in a particular category (e.g., cookies, ice cream, shampoo) and the manufacturer does market research to determine levels of purchase among the target population, penetration, awareness, and usage levels.

In less sophisticated companies (or those with overwhelming market share positions), the concept of "brand of choice" is not explored and the decline of products that fall from brand-of-choice status can often be precipitous and without warning. Clearly, this decline could have been forecasted if the concept of "brand of choice" had been understood and probed among the target audience.

The difference in consumption between an individual firm's primary brand and its secondary and tertiary brands can be significant, with each position in the consumer's purchase wardrobe representing a very distinct usage level. Once a product has slipped from the primary position to the secondary position, the door has been opened for consumers to reevaluate the viability of the brand for their specific needs. The communication efforts of competitive products, which previously ran into a cognizance barrier with the satisfied customer, can now penetrate the perception defenses and result in a considered (replacement) purchase.

In order to test the validity of this symptom, check the medicine cabinet and shower stall in your own home and count the number of analgesic, cold product, and shampoo/conditioner products. Then chart your individual usage of those products today versus six to twelve months ago, and you will soon understand the impact of the "brand of choice" phenomenon on a particular product. In other words, you'll find that you have products on hand that have not been used up but have been supplanted by other products.

SYMPTOM 10: *New products/items appear to be cannibalizing existing items from both a retailer and consumer purchase standpoint.*

Symptom 8 reflected a situation whereby expense reductions resulted in the elimination of or reduction in R&D and new product development, foreshadowing a decline in the company's future revenues. Alternatively, some companies need a turnaround for just the opposite reason. Those firms have developed new products, without doing the proper segmentation and product positioning analyses. The unfortunate result is the introduction of a new product that cannibalizes the volume of the existing brand.

Considering the cost of developing and introducing a new product and/or line extension, a company that steals consumers from one of its profitable, existing products is in effect "rearranging the deck chairs on the Titanic." In many instances, it takes anywhere from one to three years for a new product to break even, given the heavy up-front requirements for awareness and trial vehicles. A new product that is going to compete directly with the company's existing brand—one that has moved beyond the heavy up-front investment stage and crossed into profitability—ends up being a double negative for a company.

This symptom is usually a direct result of the internal organizational structure within a given company, whereby individual marketing units are encouraged to compete with one another and may report to two different bosses. Each unit is trying to secure the same customer and therefore the existing brands within the market segment are the "enemy" regardless of which flag they bear.

In yet another scenario, the marketing units report to the same boss, but the necessary consumer research and segmentation work was not done or was done incorrectly, with Symptom 10 as the result. A company that is experiencing this phenomenon is headed for trouble, because it is at once diluting one established, profitable business, while developing another (initially) unprofitable business.

Symptom 10 can also rear its ugly head at the trade (versus the consumer) level. In this instance, the firm has created a new product or products that encroach on the position of one of the firm's existing products, thus forcing the retailer to choose one over the other.

An additional negative result of introducing a new product against one of your existing brands is that the retailer will believe one or more of the following:

- Your current (existing) brand has peaked and the firm believes it is vulnerable to attack; therefore you have decided to provide consumers with another choice.
- You are placing your emphasis and consumer support behind the new product; therefore it may be time for the trade to reduce support of your existing brand which competes in the same market.
- The new product has the more current, state-of-the-art technology, rendering your existing brand "old" and soon to become obsolete in the eyes of the trade (e.g., Nintendo 16-bit machines versus the 8-bit machines).

In any event, firms that fail to recognize the conditions mentioned in Symptom 10 will have a hard time maintaining a leadership position and further will make the return-on-investment process that much harder due to the cannibalization effect.

SYMPTOM 11: *The company's manufacturing facilities are operating at less than 60 percent of capacity and future projected increases in the unit volume base are less than 10 percent of the current year volume.*

This is the final symptom of the firm in need of a turnaround and is perhaps the most potentially crippling. The manufacturing overhead level or burden in a company is usually computed by allocating the total expense to operate the facility over the forecasted number of units for the given fiscal year. Once the manufacturing overhead level is established, the firm cannot drop below the forecasted volume level or the expense of running the facility eats the profit.

Further, the cost of running a facility at 60 percent capacity is not that much different from running it at 100 percent. The costs of senior management, rent, property taxes, machinery depreciation, amortization, and the like are relatively fixed within the company's budget. Therefore, the more a firm can defray its fixed expenses, the more profitable it will be. When a firm begins running at 60 percent or less than capacity, it must quickly re-evaluate whether the entity needs to be downsized or whether the unit volume level is an aberration.

When the volume base of manufacturing facilities/organizations declines, the firm must make major cutbacks to recover the negative variance in manufacturing expense. Often these cutbacks involve elements that are critical to the marketing mix or that would contribute heavily to the growth, success, or viability of the company. The accuracy of the assessment regarding the reduced level of volume can thus mean the difference between the success and failure of a specific company.

Figure 1 is a review of the symptoms.

1. Firm is losing money from an operating profit standpoint.

2. Market share declined steadily for 12-24 months.

3. Quality managers are leaving with a degree of regularity.

4. Company pride and idea flow are greatly diminished.

5. Company facilities appear run down and quality standards seem to have declined.

6. The company is having a hard time generating—or is eating—cash.

7. On-hand inventory is out of mix with retail sales and exceeds the normal month's supply level.

8. Expense reductions have led to cutbacks in R&D, new products, and advertising and promotional spending.

9. Product or company is no longer "brand of choice."

10. New items appear to be cannibalizing existing items.

11. Manufacturing facility is operating at less than 60% of capacity and future increases are projected at less than 10% of present year.

FIGURE 1

THE SYMPTOMS

3

THE TURNAROUND PRESCRIPTION

Throughout this chapter, the reader will encounter the term "turnaround team" in conjunction with many of the principles explained in the following sections.

For purposes of this book and because every troubled company must have a select group of individuals spearheading the effort to reverse the fortunes of the firm and help it reach higher, less turbulent ground, the term turnaround team will be defined as follows:

A group of senior-level line and staff management executives singularly committed to the task of effecting the turnaround of a troubled company through the analysis, creation, implementation, and monitoring of a series of action steps, which lead to an increase in profitability (at the very least) and an overall growth of the revenue base coincident to an improvement in the manufacturing efficiency, new product development, and general morale base of the candidate company (in the best-case scenario).

Clearly, the "turnaround team" may also include members from outside the company such as consulting teams. In the case of Odyssey Partners, L.P. in some of my previous turnaround activities and Trefoil Capital Partners in the situation at L.A. Gear, the investor group team can have a profound managerial impact on the turnaround by being integrally involved in the management of the company. Whatever its composition, in a turnaround situation the "team" must function almost as a S.W.A.T unit, moving at a very high rate of speed. Members must constantly update each other on the status, progress, and new information related to the specific areas each team member is responsible for.

Further, although the team approach is clearly the most effective way to implement a turnaround, there has to be a clear and unchallenged team "captain," who has the final word after hearing all of the input and who has the full support of the entire turnaround team in implementing that decision, regardless of whether it may have differed from the individual recommendation of certain team members.

What follows in this section of the book are ten prescriptions designed to help resuscitate a dying or ailing company. Ultimately, the efficacy of the prescriptions will "live" or "die" based upon the proficiency, commitment, and communication skills of the turnaround team, for it is the human element that is frequently the difference between a successful, lasting turnaround and one that is often labeled "the quick fix."

℞ 1: *Stop the bleeding.*

In almost every turnaround situation there is a division, product line, operating facility, or "corporate project" that is losing money or draining cash at an accelerated speed. For a variety of reasons (sometimes political), these situations remain unaddressed, while vital functions are dramatically underfunded. The turnaround team must apply the tourniquet and immediately stop the continuous outflow of cash.

The problem does not always surface so readily as in the case of the "corporate project," something that is important to a senior executive but may not make financial sense. The key operating heads of functional areas must be summoned for a review of departmental expenditures to determine where the outflows are occurring and the importance of each outflow to the revenue/earnings stream.

In this first phase, the turnaround team is trying to catch the tiger by the tail to slow down the rate of decline. In some instances, a total spending shutdown must be implemented, the so-called "big drawer" theory, until the critical culprit(s) can be identified.

Often, the shutting down of spending within a troubled company serves as a calming device, enabling managers to get off the treadmill and start making smart business decisions. Negative inertia can be a crippling influence upon a company in trouble and when it impacts on the outflow of cash, disaster is not very far in the future. Therefore, "stopping the bleeding" is the first step towards getting a handle on the situation and setting a new tone within the troubled company.

One of the unfortunate side effects of the spending shutdown strategy is the prevailing feeling that there is a total lack of confidence and/or trust in the ability of the middle managers to act in a financially responsible manner. This is virtually unavoidable, however, and is one of the things that makes the task a trying exercise. In most cases, the initial problems caused by the spending shutdown or shift in the authorization process are temporary. As soon as there is an improvement in expense control and apparent deficiencies in the former system begin to be corrected, the negative aspects of the move will dissipate. Further, the reinstatement of spending authorization to middle management can be viewed as a reward/restoration of confidence and is typically met with a higher degree of importance—that is, usually taken much more seriously than before—by those who helped to create the problem in the first place.

Companies can save millions of dollars by adopting the stop-the-bleeding process. Effective implementation of this strategy sets the new corporate tone for the way things will operate and helps to promote the "corporate catharsis" that must take place among incumbent managers to make the effort a success.

R 2: *Adopt a cash management policy.*

There is no more precious corporate asset than cash. When undertaking a turnaround, strict cash management policies must be implemented whereby all expenditures over a certain level (say $1,000) must be authorized by the treasurer/controller, the executive in charge of the functional area, and the CEO or individual presiding over the turnaround. This is an extension of the stop-the-bleeding discussion described in Prescription 1 and is a practical, quick-results way to instill a cash management philosophy within a turnaround candidate.

It is amazing how many nonessential items die in their tracks when this process is instituted, because the lower- and middle-management group will think twice before sending forward an expenditure that they could previously approve by themselves on an "unaudited" basis.

Traditionally, very few companies have enlisted the services of key departmental executives in the pursuit of an overall corporate strategy. These executives often do not look beyond their individual departments and therefore do not take into account whether their expenditures are truly for the good of the firm or whether they are simply for the good of the department. But it is critical that they take an overall perspective because team management is in most cases the only way to dig the firm out of a mess quickly. A clear understanding and endorsement of the overall corporate strategy is essential to this "global" viewpoint on the part of the management team.

If the overall cash needs of the organization are properly articulated to the management group and saving cash is made a desired and admired task, most individuals will strive to achieve that goal. By having senior managers review cash expenditures over a specified level, the awareness of the cash management policy will be significantly heightened. Ultimately, when authority is returned to the departmental managers, overall cash management will be sharply improved.

R 3: *Accumulate data.*

The turnaround team must talk to everyone in the firm who can supply needed information and should take copious notes on the thoughts and perspectives of the management ranks. Always ask the question: "If you did not have to worry about what any of your bosses thought, what would you do to fix the business?" The answers will startle you with their clarity and apparent distance from the plans that are actually being implemented. This same exercise must also be conducted with key retailers, suppliers, and—in the case of an LBO or highly leveraged operation—the financial institutions and/or bondholder universe.

There is no effective way to analyze the current problems plaguing a firm and plot a successful turnaround plan without sufficient qualitative and/or quantitative data on the troubled entity. In many cases the company will not have sufficient reports, tracking studies, industry trend analyses, or other crucial studies and so the ability of the turnaround management team to extract valuable information from the heads of the work force/supplier universe will provide the analytical database.

The extraction or generation of critical data requires a skill that is foreign to many high-powered, take-charge managers: the ability to listen to others. In the zeal to show themselves as the savior of the business, the natural inclination is to espouse the turnaround strategy almost immediately, only to find out later that initial plans must be modified because of the emergence of new data. This critical shift in strategy can have an adverse effect on the psyche of the company and can lead employees to believe they are either "victims" or "culprits." It is critical for the turnaround team to disarm this syndrome by enabling everyone to feel that their input is valuable and will be viewed with a nonjudgmental eye.

The turnaround team must have the ability to both listen to employees and involve existing managers, while not losing the sense of urgency and authority that is required to lead the troops through this difficult process. In many cases, it is also appropriate to call in an outside market research or consulting firm to help analyze existing data and assist managers in compiling effective reports. These data become the foundation of the strategy formulation phase of the turnaround.

R 4: *Determine who is going to play.*

Once the turnaround team has stopped the bleeding, put the "checkbook in their own hands," and gathered the facts about the company, it is time to determine who is going to play on the team. Many people cannot shed the emotional baggage of having worked in a declining business environment and will forever doubt the new team's (or any team's) ability to turn the business around. These people constitute a "cancer" that must be excised immediately in order to create the proper environment for new, fresh thinking required to drive a troubled business.

Alternatively, an existing manager who is committed to the new cause is one of the most valuable assets any turnaround team can have. These individuals are the archive for the company; they understand the procedural issues involved with getting things done and provide the experience base that is specific to the firm so that previous mistakes will not be repeated by unsuspecting new managers.

Unfortunately, most of us consider ourselves to be great judges of character and therefore tend to shortcut the investigative and evaluative phase of the personnel process. In many cases, the outward appearance of commitment camouflages an employee's true feelings and the individual is incorrectly presumed to be "on board." In other instances, individuals who seem to be recalcitrant are actually high-spirited, caring employees who can express disagreement with a directional edict from management but will then follow it without showing or feeling any ill will. The process of deciding who is to be on the largely an issue of philosophy and chemistry, both of w specific to the individuals involved and clearly not subject to any hard and fast rules.

It is important to create a venture-team environment, whereby traditional interdepartmental barriers are broken and the crossflow of information is facilitated and encouraged. But in any case, a high degree of commitment on the part of all employees is essential. Unhappy or unsupportive workers become like a virus, and their negative attitude can be especially contagious to tired, frustrated, or vulnerable co-workers.

The venture-team concept draws on the "best available athlete" theory applied by professional sports teams during the draft process. It operates under the belief that two (or more) heads are better than one, and that bright, informed workers in an organization may have more to offer than their specific job function allows them to contribute. While it is especially critical to avoid turning the organization into a collection of generalists, the concept of managerial interaction and critique can create a stimulating, high-powered environment with effects that typically last far beyond the turnaround crisis period. The new culture of the company and the interaction between co-workers creates a sense of mutual accomplishment at having guided the firm through a troubled period. The performance and attitudes of companies that have gone through a turnaround or restructuring become more committed and participative.

One of the most effective tools a turnaround manager can utilize to determine commitment of a specific worker is to ask the key question cited in Prescription 3: "If you did not have to worry about what your bosses thought, what would you do to fix this business?" The answer to this question is valuable in the absolute (and thus provides a critical element in the data accumulation phase) and is also telling from a personal standpoint. Answers will run the gamut from specific action steps required to right the business to expressions of personal gripes (sometimes valid) directed at either specific individuals, management, or the company in general. It is the latter type of responses that must be closely watched for signs of frustration and lack of commitment that can undermine the turnaround process.

℞ 5: *Assess manufacturing capabilities.*

The manufacturing facilities in many corporations are the most valuable and underutilized assets. Unfortunately, they rarely benefit from the kind of creative thinking that typifies the marketing, promotion, and R&D functions. An analysis of corporate manufacturing capabilities in a macro sense can help achieve the following:

- Reduce overall risk of new product introductions.
- Create viable long-term alternatives to large capital expenditures on new, long-lead-time tooling.
- Provide the ability to reach the market quickly, while the new product idea is still timely or "hot."
- Improve the total cash flow to the business while helping to increase return on investment.

In effect, a company in a turnaround mode that is in need of fresh, new business should create a new-products program based upon the analysis of the existing, untapped potential of the current manufacturing base. The Corporate Capabilities Matrix is a methodology for performing this type of analysis that will be discussed in detail in Chapter 10.

The Corporate Capabilities Matrix (CCM) is designed to help analyze all of the various product categories that existing manufacturing equipment can produce. The CCM was developed while I was president of Fabergé USA, Inc. and helped the firm develop several major new products and line extensions over a relatively short eighteen-month period.

During this period the firm developed and introduced Cut-Guard Shaving Cream, McGregor Cologne, Aqua Net Non-Aerosol Hair Spray, Just Wonderful Shampoo and Conditioner, Extra-Strength Brut 33 Deodorant/Anti-Perspirant, Power Stick Deodorant/Anti-Perspirant, Fabergé European Salon Formula Shampoo, Conditioner, and Hair Spray, and the Tenax line of haircare products.

All of these products, with the exception of Power Stick Deodorant/Anti-Perspirant, were developed using existing packaging molds and filling equipment, though new graphic designs, brand names, and formulations were created. A firm the size of Fabergé in 1987–88 ($250 million) could not have developed and introduced such an impressive array of products on such a short development cycle without the development and implementation of the CCM.

Existing tooling is listed along the left side of the matrix by classification (e.g., liquid filling equipment, aerosol pressure fillers, and injection blow molding), and all of the product categories that equipment can be used for are listed across the top of the matrix. Available categories become evident through analysis of the matrix. The marketing department can then conduct segmentation, positioning, and need-gap analyses and attempt to prioritize the products that would provide the best incremental volume opportunities the most quickly. The next steps would be to develop a brand name, positioning, and formulation for the product, and then to do the requisite market research testing. This type of product development allows the firm to realize tremendous return on minimal investment because:

- The firm has the knowledge to effectively operate the production equipment required to produce the product.

- The firm avoids the major tooling investment typically associated with a new product introduction which results in a high cost of goods due to the amortization.

- Use of existing tooling enables the firm to significantly reduce the lead time required to introduce a new product.

- The firm can invest the majority of its new product funding in advertising and promotion and still realize a shorter payback period.

℞ 6: *Create the playbook.*

The time is now ripe for creating the master plan that will guide the company out of its trouble and into calmer waters. The turnaround team has been assembled and has the necessary information, along with the vision, direction, and a clear understanding of the parameters and time frame associated with the task.

The playbook is the master plan that the organization will use to execute the turnaround. It lists as well the critical checkpoints that must be part of the overall plan. Unless every individual in the company understands what he or she is supposed to do, the plan cannot succeed no matter how well conceived it is.

The playbook should include a mission statement explaining where the company is, where it is going, and its ultimate objectives, as well as a clear statement of strategies and tactics. It should also include value analysis, manufacturing procedural changes, critical path timetables for key projects, and clear assignment of responsibilities to specific individuals along with specific completion dates.

Senior managers and the turnaround team can use the playbook as a discussion vehicle for weekly status or update meetings to chart the progress of the organization in realizing the specific objectives of the turnaround plan.

R 7: *Set realistic goals.*

In football terminology the business concept of setting realistic goals would translate into "making first downs before you try to score touchdowns." Teams that move the ball down the field with consistency acquire confidence that ultimately leads them to go for the big strike, knowing that if it doesn't work, they can still move the ball down the field at a slower, more gradual rate.

The same principle works in corporations. Turnaround situations require confidence building among the incumbent managers. Accordingly, the management group must set realistic near-term goals to build confidence in the work force and in the overall plan. If in the process of following the realistic plan an unexpected opportunity presents itself, the organization will have the ability to effectively execute a "preemptive" strike, because they have already begun to realize success in what they have been doing.

Many company managers or owners, who predicted their debt service payments based on volume and profit projections that were unrealistically high, find that poor planning, forecasting, and goal setting have placed them in the unenviable position of producing revenues and profits that may seem respectable in the absolute, but come far short of the levels required to service their debt. Some of these firms have been forced into Chapter 11 bankruptcy because there was no way sales and profits could rise enough to meet the interest payments. Unfortunately, these firms may once have been vital entities, but improper planning and the inability to set realistic goals have cost them the chance to continue operating as a vital going concern.

The aforementioned examples highlight the "draconian" pitfalls associated with lack of realistic goal setting. More common problems are associated with a lack of realistic goal setting that directly relates to the internal tasks of the company. Most managers are motivated by three very basic goals:

- An increase in direct compensation
- An increase in responsibility via promotion or some similar outwardly measurable expression of superior performance
- Public or managerial recognition of a job well done that was a direct result of individual achievement

Maslow's Need Hierarchy categorized job satisfaction in similar categories (ego gratification, compensation, increased responsibility, etc.). The human ego is the driving force in almost everyone, and management of the ego is a full-time job of both the "owners" and the "influencers."

It is common to see major corporations set unrealistically high expectations of their employees in their MBOs (management by objective) and profit plans. Setting a sales growth level of 30 percent in a business where the competition is nowhere near that level and the company itself did not achieve that level in the previous year can be a demoralizing factor. The management team and work force may give up before the game has started because they feel there is no plausible way to win. Alternatively, of course, if the company achieves a 25 percent sales growth level when its previous year's growth level was 15 percent and the industry average growth rate is 5 percent, there is ample reason to expect its management and work force to rejoice and be handsomely rewarded. However, if the unrealistic goal was a 30 percent growth level, the individuals feel like they have failed and reap none of the economic and psychological benefits of a job well done. Unrealistic goals can absolutely ruin a company, because when high-achieving, ego-driven managers cannot find the proper level of fuel to continue feeding that their ego needs, they are likely to make one of three choices:

- Shut down entirely and give in to their frustration, becoming a negative influence upon the rest of the firm.
- Reduce their level of commitment to the firm in the belief that they cannot realistically expect reward levels commensurate with performance.
- Leave the firm, creating a job void as well as the feeling among remaining co-workers that a valuable member of the organization has "opted for greener pastures" and may know something they do not know.

The corporate psyche of a turnaround "patient" is so fragile that the proper translation of accomplishment/reward criteria may very well prove to be the difference between success and failure. The turnaround team must attempt to build confidence and momentum quickly if the "playbook" is to be properly translated and executed. Any ambiguity or unanswered frustration on the part of management or the work force regarding the expectations/ reward structure associated with the turnaround task can prove to be devastating to the effort.

Many LBOs include extensive equity participation for the senior managers and some equity participation for middle-level managers, because the owners of the firm believe that if the company's employees have a defined ownership stake, they will be motivated to achieve their goals and will feel the ego satisfaction that is so critical if the company's growth plan is to be sustained.

R 8: *Create an idea-generating process.*

Perhaps the most valuable asset in successful companies is the ability of people at all levels to use their knowledge, creativity, and experience to generate ideas. These companies set up systems that encourage, if not demand, personnel at all levels to submit topical ideas on a regular (often weekly) basis. Idea generation enables everyone in the firm to believe he or she has a direct voice in determining the organization's future, and it can also help to uncover hidden "jewels" within the company.

Ideas that are ultimately implemented should be rewarded and the initiator or inventor, co-workers involved in the execution, and the individual's boss who helped to direct and/or carry out the plan should all be compensated. It is amazing where ideas come from, and how close some of them are to the needs of the consumer target audience that the firm is trying to reach. Another benefit is that ideas generated internally by employees in functional areas related to the manufacturing process tend to be very cost effective and in many cases improve the firm's overall economies of scale.

To maximize the idea-generating process, a company should create a clearly defined system that employees at all levels can understand. The system should delineate the means by which ideas should be submitted (oral, written, etc.) and the method with which an idea will be evaluated, along with an approximate time frame for the employee to expect a response. And the method for compensating the individual and supporting cast should be clearly explained to avoid ambiguities and possible negative consequences after adoption of the idea in terms of financial reward expectations.

A viable idea-generating system is an absolute must when a company is operating in a turnaround mode. Financial and operational issues can often overwhelm senior management from a time management standpoint, and new ideas tend to slow down considerably due to a preoccupation with addressing the potentially "life threatening" issues.

Unfortunately, when a firm goes through a turnaround and finally emerges from under the dark cloud of financial/operational constraints, the newly streamlined organization finds itself further behind the market than it was previously, because new initiatives had been put on hold during the crisis management period. The situation can become more dangerous because a small group of senior executives with a given group of issues dominates the entire organization, whether or not the middle and lower management people are directly involved with those issues. In effect, people stop thinking and become preoccupied with doing, and that can be a grave mistake when going through the turnaround process.

Once a company and its management realize that the human capital within an organization is usually its most valuable asset, systems designed to maximize the productivity and value of those assets should be pursued with the same vigor as those devised for the hard assets of the company. In addition, once members of the work force understand that their ideas are going to be solicited on a regular basis and that they will have a non-hierarchical forum in which to express those ideas, the entire psyche of the firm will change and the pride and possessiveness we referred to back in Symptom 4 of Chapter 2 will surface.

Further discussion of the internal idea-generating process and reward system will be discussed in Chapter 12, "Value Engineering."

℞ 9: *Create a war chest.*

Within any turnaround situation, generating cash is the most vital element in the process, because the cash can be used to pay bills, fund new ideas, and create the flexibility to respond to specific needs and trends as they present themselves.

Firms in a turnaround mode often go into Chapter 11 or a prepackaged bankruptcy, and encounter significant difficulties receiving merchandise from vendors or suppliers, who are justifiably uncertain about the ability of the troubled firm to pay its bills. More often than not, suppliers will place the firm on a COD basis to read their ability to pay over a given period before returning to normal trade/credit terms.

A firm that is approaching bankruptcy should begin to hoard cash, even at the risk of elongating vendor payment cycles or seeking special terms. Countless numbers of firms that are best categorized as "busted LBOs" have moved into the Chapter 11 mode and yet possess an inordinate amount of cash on their balance sheets. Further, because of the nature of the Chapter 11 process and the leniency of creditors, these firms will typically amass cash at an accelerated rate.

A firm that is well managed through the turnaround process and is under Chapter 11 bankruptcy protection may well emerge much stronger than it was in its previous life, with a well-proportioned balance sheet, improved liquidity, and the ability to move at a higher rate of speed. On the other hand, many firms that are nowhere near the threat of Chapter 11 are definitely turnaround candidates. These firms typically have a much more difficult problem to manage, because they lack the safe haven of Chapter 11, and the ability to negotiate within their vendor base. In these situations, the firm must begin a cash management program immediately in order to gain control of this scarce and precious asset.

As discussed in Prescription 2 (adopt a cash management policy), the systems that a firm puts in place when entering the turnaround mode should be heavily geared towards the generation and control of cash flow. However, Prescription 9 is different from Prescription 2 because the ''war chest'' is used to take advantage of opportunistic developments in the market. The war chest creates an image of a firm that has money to spend at a time when the market has judged it to be ''in trouble.'' This is a very effective means of changing both investor and trade opinions vis-à-vis the troubled firm.

For example, if a business has hit hard times because of the dated image of its products, perceived functional obsolescence, or lack of market penetration, that firm could use its cash war chest to purchase a brand that could be run through its existing (efficient) manufacturing facility. This method of acquiring ''strategic'' volume helps the firm to achieve the following:

- Immediate market presence/penetration in a particular business segment, where the product characteristics are similar to those currently manufactured by the firm.

- Realization of manufacturing efficiencies and overhead recovery through the increased volume in the plant against a fixed burden rate.

- Ability to get to market quickly without the usual timing constraints associated with the new product development process.

- Investment of live cash into a known entity with a proven

track record as opposed to investment in an entirely new product that may never be successful.

This strategy would not be feasible for a troubled firm with a low cash position, because the capital markets would not be eager to finance a highly leveraged purchase of an intangible asset (a brand) for a firm whose financial position is questionable. Accumulation of cash can lead to greater credibility, and possible growth of a new brand. As the slogan for the 1990s suggests: Cash is king!

Ŗ 10: *Show demonstrable progress.*

The tenth and final prescription is perhaps the most critical element in the entire turnaround process because it involves showing measurable headway against predetermined performance objectives.

The credibility of the turnaround team rests with their ability to motivate the organization through the creation of a winning feeling and the notion that troubled times are behind and better times are ahead. During the turnaround mode, many individuals inside the company work inordinately long hours on a short-handed basis to help execute plans and programs they may not necessarily agree with. In effect, the members of the organization have "bought in" to the plans created and directed by the turnaround team, which is usually a significant departure from where the firm operated previously.

It is important to the success of the project that specific measurable criteria for evaluating the progress be agreed to before executing the plan. It is up to the turnaround team to ensure that a majority of those objectives are met within the turnaround process.

There is nothing like success to convert anxious employees into devoted zealots. No matter how committed the incumbent managers seem in the beginning of the turnaround process, invariably human nature takes over and the Missouri Syndrome ("show me") penetrates the psyche of the troops. Only when all members of the organization begin to see clear signs of progress and achievement of stated business goals will they begin to feel that the plan is sound, viable, and moving along on track. The tension and fear within the troubled company will gradually dissipate and will be replaced by a new entrepreneurial spirit.

Often the senior members of the management team forget how fragile the corporate psyche is and how good news does not always travel vertically. Specifically, while the senior management may be aware of specific accomplishments, the word is often not passed down to the people who would benefit most from hearing it. The worst thing that can happen to a company that seems to be picking up momentum in the marketplace is to have employees be the last to know and feel that they were being used as pawns during the turnaround process, but are not being viewed as "partners" during the success mode.

It is imperative that throughout the turnaround period, weekly or biweekly meetings are held with senior managers to keep them informed about demonstrable progress. In turn, they should meet with members of their departments to share the news. Keeping the internal organization well informed throughout the process will help to create both a groundswell effect as well as an esprit de corps, which will help to propel the company's turnaround plan.

Depending upon the specific problems that were facing the troubled entity before the turnaround process began, a number of specific goals should be established as the evidence of demonstrable progress as defined by Prescription 10:

- Improvement in the absolute level of operating profit
- Improvement in the operating profit/gross margin levels
- Increase in market share
- Improvement in information flow within the company
- Reduction in the new product development lead time

- Creation of an internal idea-generating process
- Increase in sales
- Increased utilization of existing production capacity
- Penetration of incremental business segments
- Resuscitation of an existing business in decline
- Increase in level of internal promotions
- Improvement in accessibility of top management
- Reduction or elimination of internal political system
- Expanded distribution of product line
- Increased level of trade support

This list is representative of the kinds of accomplishments that would show demonstable progress to the organization and dramatically improve the overall attitude of the work force and increase their confidence in both the management team and the future of the company.

Figure 2 reviews the prescriptions.

1. Stop the bleeding.
2. Adopt a cash management policy.
3. Accumulate data.
4. Determine who is going to play.
5. Assess manufacturing capabilities.
6. Create the playbook.
7. Set realistic goals.
8. Create an idea-generating process.
9. Create a war chest.
10. Show demonstrable progress.

FIGURE 2

THE PRESCRIPTIONS

PART II

ENGINEERING A MARKETING TURNAROUND: CONCEPTS AND CASES

4

The Marketing Turnaround Blueprint

The eleven symptoms and ten prescriptions described in Part I of this book deal with companies that are for the most part in need of a total turnaround. While there are many in that category, there are a great many others whose problems are almost solely marketing related. In some instances the firm's brands have "fallen from grace," or the firm has lost its focus and allowed precious intangible and tangible assets to deteriorate over time.

A marketing turnaround involves the reassessment of existing products within the company as well as the total image of the firm itself and determining how best to leverage those assets to create franchise growth.

Enormous rewards can be derived from conducting a successful marketing turnaround if the firm can find a way to effectively attract new users to the brand or company without disenfranchising current users. Financial rewards can be achieved swiftly and in significant proportions if both markets are considered.

I have been directly involved with the marketing turnarounds of eight different companies during the 1983–1991 period including:

- Revlon Fragrance & Skincare Division
- Fabergé USA, Incorporated
- Reebok International Ltd.
- Revell/Monogram Incorporated
- Eagle Food Centers
- Black Box Corporation
- Catalina Swimwear
- Cole of California

At Revlon, Fabergé, and Reebok I served in top executive positions (vice president of worldwide marketing, president, and chief marketing officer, respectively), whereas the turnarounds of Revell/Monogram, Eagle Food Centers, Black Box Corporation, and Taren Holdings Corporation were conducted by the Odyssey Partners, L.P. Internal Operating Unit, a five-man team of former top executives, all principals of Odyssey, and me. As members of that unit, we were responsible for managing the companies through some very difficult times and the CEOs of those firms worked directly with our unit.

The firms listed above which have successfully gone through the marketing turnaround process are extremely diverse. The group includes a $2.5 billion beauty care company (Revlon), a $400 million toiletries/fragrance company (Fabergé), a $1.5 billion athletic footwear company (Reebok), a $110 million toy/hobby kit company (Revell/Monogram), a $1.3 billion midwest

regional supermarket chain (Eagle Food Centers), a $125 million
high-tech data communications direct mail firm (Black Box
Corp.), and a $300 million apparel conglomerate consisting of
two of the largest swimwear manufacturers in the United States
(Cole of California and Catalina) and one of the largest private
label knitwear/sportswear manufacturers in the country (Colonial
Corporation of America).

THE MARKETING TURNAROUND BLUEPRINT

The marketing turnaround blueprint is a comprehensive step-by-
step process designed to help managers analyze the true potential
of a specific business. While the blueprint is ideally suited to
companies with branded products or services, its versatility is
such that it can be applied to a broad range of businesses. Part II
will review the marketing turnaround blueprint in detail and attempt to show that the stepwise system is adaptable to virtually
any business involved in selling a product to the ultimate consumer.

**A marketing turnaround refers to the transformation of
one or more brands within a corporation for purposes of
regenerating or extending the product life cycle to include
a return to the growth phase.**

Simply stated, the marketing turnaround process can be applied
to a variety of companies and/or products whose current level
of vitality and viability is significantly less than it was at a
point in the recent past. Such companies may be viewed as
"tired," with dated product and advertising imagery; their
product line(s) may be perceived as technologically obsolete; or
a lack of true marketing and/or product innovation may have

relegated the firm to "me too" status, which is the precursor to marketing oblivion.

As explained in Part I, "Diagnostics," which relate in large part to the total turnaround process, cash management, asset allocation, and the like, do not come into play in the marketing turnaround blueprint. Therefore, the marketing turnaround blueprint can be carried out by a middle-level manager, because the nature of the activities and the scope of responsibility and authority required to execute it are well within the scope of a middle manager's role.

WHO IS RIPE FOR A MARKETING TURNAROUND?

Any company or brand which has previously exhibited a level of sales volume which made it a factor within given segments of the consumer marketplace is ripe for a marketing turnaround.

Included in this category may be brands that were significant players within a specific market segment or entire companies whose line of products or brands collectively represented a meaningful level of volume within single or multiple market segments.

It is very important to determine right from the beginning whether or not the entity is in fact ripe for a marketing turnaround. For example, if a product was introduced into the market but over time never really became successful or developed a core user following, that entity is not a candidate for a marketing turnaround per se, because the product never achieved the requisite saliency level referred to above.

The marketing turnaround blueprint is not a magical formula designed to ensure product success from dismal failure. It is an analytical framework designed to help highlight aspects of a company and/or brand that can be leveraged, and to attempt to use sophisticated segmentation and product positioning tools to help create a viable future for the entity. When done correctly, the marketing turnaround can create enormous value from existing assets, both tangible and intangible, with excellent economics and expediency.

WHAT IS THE FIRST STEP IN ENGINEERING A MARKETING TURNAROUND?

When determining the proper first step in conducting a marketing turnaround it is critical for the turnaround team to decide whether the turnaround is to be conducted on the entire company or on a specific brand or product. The techniques vary significantly depending upon the scope of the turnaround and the focus of the effort.

Conducting a Corporate Marketing Turnaround

When the turnaround candidate is an entire company and its portfolio of products, the task is obviously much more imposing and the attendant level of risk is much greater. Accordingly, when conducting a corporate marketing turnaround, the company's overall priorities play a major role in the type of program the firm will adopt and the level of risk the firm is prepared to take. In such a turnaround, the following key steps are critical to the success of the endeavor and will ultimately set the tone for the turnaround effort:

- Determine what the current profile of the company is within the marketplace from both a consumer and trade perspective.

- Evaluate the specific advantages of the company vis-à-vis competition from a marketing, sales, production, and formulation perspective and how those advantages can be leveraged to provide the company with an edge in the marketplace.
- Determine which categories the company should compete within and set realistic objectives for penetrating those segments utilizing existing brands, line extensions, and/or new products.

These three exercises constitute the first step in conducting an effective corporate marketing turnaround and will provide the basis for the rest of the markieting turnaround blueprint.

Conducting a Brand or Product Turnaround

In the situations where the turnaround task at hand is for a particular brand or product, several issues must be immediately addressed before any meaningful work can begin. The key risk factor involved with conducting such a turnaround is the potential for disenfranchising the existing user base. Many times the turnaround effort is detoured because for every new user the brand acquires, it loses an existing user. From an economic standpoint this can spell disaster, because the incremental cost of the new unit sale is far greater than the highly efficient repeat purchase.

The key elements involved in the first step of a brand or product turnaround are as follows:

- Determine the brand's unique advantage vis-à-vis competitive entries in the same segment of the market (e.g., price, performance, positioning).

- Evaluate the status of the current franchise:

  1. Is there a loyal core?

  2. Does the rate of influx approach the rate of attrition?

  3. What is the profile of the current user?

  4. Is the brand typically "brand of choice"?

- Conduct a need-gap analysis of the category:

  1. What are the emerging trends?

  2. Which of these trends could the brand capitalize upon?

  3. Will the marketing strategy involve "niche" marketing or a broad-based attack?

These are the basic building blocks of a brand or product marketing turnaround, because they help to establish the parameters in terms of vulnerability of the current volume base and the potential for delivering both new and incremental users to the franchise.

5

ANALYZING RELEVANT PRODUCT CATEGORIES

When conducting a marketing turnaround it is essential to understand the exact nature of the markets in which you are competing and the specific dynamics of those markets. In other words, a sophisticated segmentation analysis is one of the most vital tools of a marketing turnaround team and the quality of that analysis will bear directly on the potential success of the new marketing initiative.

Within the analysis of relevant product categories, the following four issues are of critical importance:

- Each category or market must be segmented by price and/or positioning to include key characteristics of major brands, the percent of category volume by subsegment, the major players in the category, and the need gaps that exist within the company's arsenal.

- The company must determine whether a vertical or horizontal penetration strategy will be used in categories where the firm has existing entries (e.g., dominate price-value or place entries in several segments).
- The effect of cannibalization must be assessed in categories where a horizontal strategy will be employed.
- The effect of systematic risk must be considered in a vertical strategy within single categories, versus a horizontal strategy involving expansion into new categories that are totally incremental to the company's mix.

ASSESSING EXISTING BRANDS

A thorough assessment of existing brands in the company's portfolio is the necessary first step in developing an effective turnaround plan. Often brands within a company have been misread or improperly positioned in an ever-changing market environment. Repositioning an existing entity without disenfranchising its existing user base is one of the most difficult tasks in the process. The marketing positioning of a specific product cannot be shifted or refined without a thorough understanding of the current user base and the level of support required to preserve that base at its existing level of volume. In assessing existing brands within the company, six key questions must be answered before the turnaround process can effectively move forward:

1. Where do the existing brands stand within the market?
2. How do the brands fit into the total corporate strategy?
3. Should the brands be repositioned, repackaged, reformulated, or line extended?
4. How do you preserve the loyal core users?

5. Should the firm invest towards growth or attempt to maintain a given volume level?

6. Are the individual brands "chiefs" (brands you invest in) or "Indians" (brands you milk for cash)?

Once the turnaround team has this information the various vulnerabilities of the individual product lines will be highlighted and the fragility of the existing volume base will be uncovered. For example, if there are five brands in the entire company and the data suggest that all of them are in a vulnerable position and will require "chief" levels of spending, and if the loyal core user bases are tenuous, the total long-term strategy of the company would need to be reassessed.

In this case the firm may decide that two of the five brands are not worth that level of expenditure given their growth potential. Those two should immediately be moved into "milk" status, and development of new products or line extensions would become the priority for utilization of the remaining funds.

Unfortunately, decisions involving the status of established brands within a company often take on emotional overtones. It is imperative that the aforementioned analysis provide all parties with an objective, factual snapshot of the existing situation. Once these data are gathered and the true status of each brand has been determined, the next phase of the marketing turnaround process involves the clear delineation of what direction the brands should be pursuing in the future, designated in this blueprint as the mission statement.

The case of Revell, Inc., which follows, exemplifies how assessing existing brands can lead to greater worth if they are updated, aligned, and "turned around" for the market.

6

REVELL, INC.

By December of 1989 Revell was the largest model/hobby kit company in the United States, featuring two major brands: Revell and Monogram. Together the two brands accounted for roughly 65 percent of the domestic model kit market and were clearly recognized as the dominant players in a declining industry. Odyssey Partners, L.P. had acquired Revell, Inc. through an LBO in 1986 and merged Revell with Monogram, the other major model kit manufacturer in the market, to create a formidable market leader. In mid-to-late 1989, it became apparent that Revell was experiencing some significant business problems, and Odyssey Partners, L.P. stepped in to assist management in addressing these problems.

From December of 1989 until June of 1990 the Odyssey turnaround team analyzed the business and created the strategic turnaround plan that would ultimately help lead Revell out of the woods and back to a position of respectable profitability. In the interim, a new head of marketing was hired and the Odyssey Internal Operating Unit was fully involved in helping to effect the turnaround of the firm.

The basic problems the company faced were as follows:

- Lack of contemporary imagery in the model/hobby kit field
- Lack of contemporary image in both packaging and the product
- Inherent bias of mothers against a glue/paint-based assembly product
- Inability of the consumer to determine the degree of difficulty in assembling the product prior to purchase
- Less than optimal rate of completion by consumers
- Lack of understanding regarding the primary purchaser/ target audience for model kits (adults, teens, or kids)
- Lack of any meaningful internal market research regarding the attitude and usage habits of category users in general and Revell/Monogram users in particular
- Overemphasis on vehicular (air, auto, ship) subject matter
- Lack of inclusion of paint/glue within the kits
- Virtually no trade advertising
- No consumer advertising
- Absence of age-specific model kits to appeal to the broadest range of potential consumers
- No point-of-sale or in-store merchandising/fixturization by the company or the retailer in support of the category or the brand

• Inability of consumers to get assembly advice and assistance when they need it

These characteristics contributed to Revell's fall in profitability in 1990 and made the need for effecting the turnaround program all the more urgent.

Basically, Odyssey's turnaround team in conjunction with management downsized the company, effectively lowering the break-even level of the firm by 25 percent, and revamped the marketing and imagery of the firm from top to bottom, including commissioning landmark research of the model kit business and consumer usage and attitudes vis-à-vis the brands and the category.

The research confirmed many of our preexisting beliefs regarding the consumer's opinion of model building, as well as the various barriers to entry and repeat purchase. The research indicated a very high awareness and "ever tried" level among boys ages ten to thirteen, but a very high frustration level as well. Issues such as the difficulty and messiness of painting and gluing of the model kits and the inability to determine the level of difficulty before purchasing were cited as major drawbacks. In the case of younger users, the major issues related to overall difficulty of assembly, lack of pride in the finished product, and the drawback associated with the glue and paint process.

The team analyzed the existing tool and mold bank at the company and attempted to create a corporate capabilities matrix to highlight the quick-strike, highly profitable leverage points available at Revell and Monogram. We found that numerous snap-together model tools had already been fully amortized some years back and were lying virtually dormant in the Revell factory. Our strategy was to take these fully amortized tools (i.e., cost of goods is low because the tooling expense is already written off) and attempt to create a highly saleable line of products to appeal to the eight- to twelve-year-old consumer who shuns a glue-based model kit.

First, we executed a strategy for creating the perfect model kit for kids, one that required no paint or glue to assemble. In the process of that investigation, we discovered a resin material that had a consistency similar to polystyrene (the material used to make model kits), but that had a phosphorescent character as well. This trait enabled the product to carry a bright neon color and to glow intensely under a black light.

The neon color and snap-together technology meant that the product did not have to be painted or glued, thus addressing the key negatives associated with model building as stated in the firm's landmark research project. We came up with the name "Luminators" and created a dynamic new box with neon photographs of the specific airplane or car contained in the box, along with a front panel offer to purchase the Luminator-Ray black light by mail. The product line featured four airplanes and four cars, all of which could be manufactured with fully amortized, virtually dormant tools, and which were able to accommodate the new resin material easily. Luminators was the perfect product to address the key weaknesses of the Revell/Monogram company in its attempt to attract new, younger users to the category. Within ninety days from the initial shipment to the retail stores, Luminators was among the leading selling model kit items in the company at several key toy retailers.

In keeping with the "no-glue" strategy to help expand the category user base, we relaunched the old SnapTite brand of airplanes, boats, cars, and trucks, using entirely new packaging and a completely new marketing thrust for the snap-together category. This was a classic example of using market research to help reassess and reposition a brand. In addition, we developed a skill-level labeling system that delineated the various difficulty levels by number of pieces and difficulty of assembly. The system was similar to the one used in the downhill ski industry (green = easy, blue = intermediate, black = expert) and the principal goal was to manage the expectations of the purchaser and ultimate user. Skiers who try a black diamond slope and find it too difficult rarely say that skiing is not for them and give up the sport. They are more likely to realize that the slope was too difficult and try a blue or green trail to determine their own proficiency level and heighten safety and enjoyment.

The same logic holds true for the model kit business. If a model kit proves too difficult for a hobbyist to assemble and its packaging indicates no scale of difficulty, the discouraged user is likely to assume that the entire model-building process is too difficult and never try another kit.

Accordingly the following system was devised for Revell and Monogram model kits to help guide consumers' purchase decisions and manage their expectations and frustrations:

- SKILL 1: SnapTite—less than 50 pieces; easy to assemble
- SKILL 2: Revell and Monogram—less than 100 pieces; moderate level of difficulty
- SKILL 3: Revell and Monogram—over 100 pieces; most difficult to assemble, expert level

The skill-level labeling was displayed prominently in the upper right-hand corner of the packaging and the complete skill-level range of Revell and Monogram products was displayed along the side panel of the boxes to encourage proficient modelers to graduate in terms of difficulty.

In addition to the Luminators, SnapTite, and skill-level labeling, Monogram introduced fresh looking, contemporized outer packaging, established a Revell/Monogram "800 number hotline," and developed an aggressive in-store merchandising/ fixturization program featuring injection molded plastic framing units for the model kit department, highlighting Revell and

Monogram products (including their skill levels), along with freestanding modular display units.

We also created the company's first television commercials featuring Luminators, SnapTite, and Revell/Monogram glue kits. The trade was indoctrinated regarding the new Revell by means of a unique trade advertising/repositioning program under the heading of "Building a 'Model' Future," that featured a slick brochure, videotape, and multipage trade advertising program. Last but not least, the company's Skillcraft line of science kit products was also repackaged and repositioned under a "lab" theme (EcoLab, MicroLab, etc.) and reintroduced to the trade during early 1991 as well.

All of these efforts resulted in dramatically improved profitability—from a loss position in 1990 to a profit approaching $8 milllion in 1991. The firm went public in an Initial Public Offering in June 1991, selling roughly three million shares of stock on the American Stock Exchange at an opening price of $9 per share or approximately $27 million.

Revell/Monogram's turnaround was quite remarkable for a company that only a year earlier seemed to have no prospect for significant near- or long-term growth in either sales or profitability. This was a classic example of how a turnaround team—in this case consisting of the management of Revell, Inc. and the Odyssey Partners, L.P. Operating Unit and Financial Principals—could take an underperforming, seemingly stagnant business and create a highly valuable, well-positioned entity that should be a solid market leader within the toy/hobby industry for many years.

7

CREATING A MISSION STATEMENT

Each company or brand must have an individual mission statement which clearly states its near-term and long-term positioning goals. Most companies do not have mission statements for their brands and this often leads to the cannibalization of one brand by another brand offered by the same company. Revell's mission statement was to provide consumers from age seven through adult with a broad spectrum of model kits (glue and snap) involving varying degrees of assembly complexity (skill levels) and decoration needs (paint/no paint required) in primarily vehicular product categories such as airplanes, cars, and ships.

The senior management of the firm should use the compilation of the individual brand mission statements to create a master mission statement for the entire organization. Further, the perusal of the various mission statements of the individual brands will help to highlight duplication of efforts, potential pitfalls, lack of breadth within a category, and other possible shortcomings.

The mission statement serves as a "flight plan" for all future marketing activities. It can be particularly effective in helping the management responsible for an individual brand to evaluate their marketing programs and determine if they are consistent with the stated direction of the brand.

Key elements to be included in any successful mission statement for a specific brand are as follows:

- Statement of the brand's positioning
- Clear delineation of the various line extensions within the brand and the specific goals of each
- Clear statement of the volume-related measures the brand intends to achieve (which may include volume levels, market share, or both)

The mission statement is the marketing equivalent of the corporate credo, in that it sets the tone for everything the brand at-

---

BRUT/BRUT 33
Mission Statement—1987

The primary focus for BRUT/BRUT 33 for the next three-year period is continued franchise growth. This will be accomplished by attracting new users into the BRUT franchise via the fragrance, the "lead horse," and then converting them into total BRUT users by luring them to the BRUT 33 line of toiletries.

Additionally, new products will be developed using new brand names authenticated by the corporate name, "BRUT." They will compete in specific fragrance markets and efficacy-driven toiletry categories where the BRUT name and image is a limiting factor.

FIGURE 3

MISSION STATEMENT

tempts to accomplish and creates something approaching a standard by which the activities of the brand should be measured. Figure 3 shows the mission statement Fabergé developed for its men's toiletry lines, Brut and Brut 33.

DEVELOPING A LINE POSITIONING MATRIX

Once the mission statement has been created, the next step in the marketing turnaround blueprint is the development of the line positioning matrix. This matrix is a tool that helps to clearly segment a brand and its line extensions and provides distinct criteria for evaluating the various marketing elements employed in an overall strategy. The principal benefit of the line positioning matrix to the management of the brand or company is that it will help to highlight the potential for direct product cannibalization by showing the possible overlapping of the positionings of a parent brand and its line extensions.

The line positioning matrix would feature the following subheadings:

- Brand
- Positioning
- Target Audience
- Segment

By analyzing the various products within the line positioning matrix, an overall brand strategy can be developed that maximizes the potential of each of the products, while maintaining a consistent overall image and a minimal amount of direct product cannibalization. Table 1 shows the line positioning matrix developed for Brut/Brut 33 products, while Tables 2 and 3 provide the category segmentation matrixes for each of the relevant Brut

TABLE   1

Brut/Brut 33
Line Positioning Matrix—1987

Brand	Positioning	Target Audience	Segment
Brut • *Cologne* • *Gift sets*	*The masculine/ manly fragrance women will like*	*–Men 18–34* *–Income less than $40M* *–High school graduate/some college* *–Blue/grey collar* *–"Macho"*	• *Mid-price men's fragrance*
Brut 33 • *Cologne* • *After shave* • *Splash-on* • *Deodorant/ Anti-pers- pirants* • *Other toiletries* • *Gift sets*	*Quality toilet- ries for men at popular prices, all with the great smell of Brut*	*–Men 18–49* *–Income less than $40M* *–High school graduate/some college* *–Blue/grey collar* *–"Macho"*	• *Men's toiletries/ fragrance- driven* • *Popular priced men's fra- grances*

and Brut 33 businesses (cologne/aftershaves and deodorant/anti-perspirants). In analyzing the two competitive segmentation matrixes (Tables 2 and 3), the line positioning matrix (Table 1) tends to have a greater meaning to the user by creating numerical parameters to the development potential for the product line in the categories in which it will compete.

TABLE 2

BRUT/BRUT 33—1987 COMPETITIVE COLOGNES/AFTER-SHAVES MATRIX

Market Size $483,000,000
Growth +17%

Segments	Popular Price	Mid Price	High Price
	Brut 33	Brut	Polo
	Old Spice	Stetson	Halston
	English Leather	Chaps	Aramis
	Aqua Velva	Jovan Musk	Pierre Cardin
	Skin Bracer	Coty Musk	
		British Sterling	

Brand	Positioning	Pricing	Estimated Share	Advertising Spending 1985 Full Year (in Millions)
Mid Price				
Brut	• Masculine/sex appeal	1.5 oz-$7.50	2%	$6.0
Stetson	• Romantic/adventurous	2.0 oz.-$8.75	6%	$6.4
Chaps	• Adventurous	1.8 oz-$10.00	5%	$3.5
Coty Musk	• Sex appeal	2.0 oz-$6.95	4%	$.9
Jovan Musk	• Sexy/masculine	1.0 oz-$7.00	6%	$2.6
British Sterling	• Romantic	2.0 oz-$6.25	2%	$1.8
Popular Price				
Brut 33	• Masculine/sex appeal	3.5 oz-$2.39	8%	—
Old Spice	• America's favorite/ for every man	4.25 oz-$4.19	13%	$7.4
English Leather	• Romantic/seductive	2.0 oz-$3.50, 4.0 oz-$6.00	6%	$4.8
Aqua Velva	• Functional/cooling	4.0 oz-$2.49	3%	$4.2
Skin Bracer	• Functional/skincare	4.0 oz-$2.39	7%	$6.6

TABLE 3

BRUT/BRUT 33–1987 COMPETITIVE
DEODORANT/ANTI-PERSPIRANTS MATRIX

Market Size $1,261,000,000
Growth +16%

Segments:	• By Form:	Sticks	Sprays	Roll-ons
		42%	28%	27%
	• By Sex:	Male	Female	Unisex
		25%	33%	36%

Male Brands	Positioning	Forms	SKU's	Estimated Share	Advertising Spending (Jan–Sept 1986, in millions)
Brut 33	• Masculine/ sex appeal efficacy	Stick Spray	7 6	4%	$ 2.6
Speed Stick	• Efficacy/ unique formula	Stick	12	10%	$12.2
Old Spice	• Efficacy/ superiority	Stick Spray	13 2	6%	$ 5.3
Right Guard	• Sex appeal/ masculinity	Stick Spray	12 6	6%	$ 4.5
English Leather	• Masculine	Stick Spray	6 2	1%	$ .5

ASSESSING THE BRAND OR COMPANY PROFILE

Because the consumer, trade, and internal perceptions of the company or brand may differ greatly, or they may be consistent but not where they need to be to significantly leverage the equity of the entity, a thorough assessment of the brand or company profile will help immeasurably in any turnaround effort. The profile of the company can be determined through the market research process, based upon an objective questionnaire designed to read the true perceptions of the interviewees. The following three perceptions must be clearly identified:

1. *Consumer Perception.* What image do consumers have of the company, and what image do they have for the brand? Are they consistent?

2. *Retailer Perception.* What does the retail community think of the company and the brand in terms of what they stand for?

3. *Internal Perception.* How does the company see itself and/or the products within the company? Does the company's perception of itself and its products differ greatly from the perceptions of the consumer and the retailer?

If the answers to those questions indicate that the perceptions of the company, the consumer, and the retailer do vary greatly, then the first thing that the company must do in the turnaround process is to help align those three perceptions. The turnaround team must determine the relative strengths of each perception and attempt to integrate those strengths into an overall updated image for the company or brand.

This step in the marketing turnaround blueprint is of critical importance, since many times the consumer perception of the product or corporate image is very different from what the actual positioning of the entity intended it to be and may, in fact, be an (intangible) asset. This can clearly be shown for a variety of products and companies which derive an undeserved benefit from consumer misperception.

Two classic examples of this beneficial misperception involve the case of a product (Head & Shoulders Shampoo) and a company (Fabergé, Inc.). The case of Head & Shoulders Shampoo involves the misperception that the product has a dual benefit of both relieving a dandruff condition and preventing dandruff from occurring. The product is absolutely designed to relieve the dandruff problem, but is not designed to help prevent the condition. Nevertheless, a large number of consumers, mostly men, use Head & Shoulders Shampoo in the hope of preventing the occurrence of dandruff, thus providing the brand with a large number of loyal users due to benefit misperception.

The case of Fabergé, Inc. was also intriguing, because a great many consumers believed that Fabergé was a brand of expensive, department store cosmetics and fine fragrances, when in fact the company manufactured no cosmetic products under the Fabergé label and marketed mass-market fragrance products sold in drug stores, such as Brut cologne and Brut 33 after-shave. This imagery had enabled Fabergé to benefit from the upscale imagery of the misconception on the part of consumers and to create a value impression for its mass-market toiletries products, which sold at very popular prices.

In the case of both Head & Shoulders and Fabergé, Inc., the identification and understanding of the differences between perception and reality helped both of those entities realize unjustifiable benefits that millions of dollars of advertising and promotion may never have provided.

8

DETERMINING THE SPECIFIC ADVANTAGES OF THE COMPANY

In order to create an effective marketing turnaround plan for a specific company, the turnaround team must attempt to differentiate the product or company from the competition. In marketing circles this is often referred to as creating a unique selling proposition, but in the case of an entire company rather than a specific product, the differentiation may take the form of a process or discipline advantage that separates the firm from the competition.

Given that the breadth of products we could discuss is almost infinitely diverse and the criteria for developing a unique selling proposition are specific to each product, we will focus here on the ways to determine the specific advantages a company may possess that can be leveraged to provide a competitive edge in the marketplace.

There are four key areas to examine when attempting to determine the specific advantages of a company in the business of manufacturing and marketing a product to the consumer public:

- Production/manufacturing
- Sales
- Research and development
- Marketing

PRODUCTION/MANUFACTURING

Production/manufacturing is a very powerful tool to maintain as a competitive advantage in the consumer marketplace, because with it comes the financial leverage of low-cost production, ability to mass produce on a shortened cycle, and the ability to manufacture a unique process. When determining whether or not the firm is going to be able to use the production area as a point of competitive leverage, the following questions must be answered:

- Is the company a low-cost producer?
- Does the company possess production facilities or techniques that are unique within that industry?
- Does the company possess production flexibility that makes it able to get product to market faster?
- Is the company completely vertically integrated so that they not only manufacture the product itself, but also the primary packaging which contains the product?

If the company possesses one or more of the above characteristics vis-à-vis the production process, that may well be the platform for the creation of a powerful advantage within the market, which can become the cornerstone for a marketing turnaround strategy.

SALES

The sales function is often overlooked in the process of taking an inventory of corporate leverage points, because on the surface it appears to be an unscientific discipline that is almost entirely based upon human (versus mechanistic or process) capital. The notion that a good salesperson is someone who has been blessed with "the gift of gab" and the ability to make small talk with total strangers is an outdated stereotype that unjustly underestimates the effective methods employed by many organizations and their salespeople to achieve a competitive advantage.

The sales function in a company is perhaps the most critical element in the near-term success of the entity, because without an effective sales organization, all of the great ideas in the world will never get to market. A strategic, disciplined approach to account management and creating a systematic approach to presenting a company and its products to the trade can lay the groundwork for many successful periods of sales and profit growth. This continuity of message ultimately helps to create the personality of the firm in the eyes of the retailer universe.

Many times, smaller entrepreneurial firms who are having trouble achieving effective levels of retail distribution are purchased by larger, structured, more disciplined companies, whose sales organizations can achieve dramatic increases in penetrating the retail trade. Some of these benefits relate to the sheer size and breadth of the sales organization, but often times it is the approach the firm takes to selling a product within its line that provides the competitive advantage.

Asking three key questions may determine if the sales function of a particular company is a source for competitive advantage:

- Is the sales force or broker (manufacturer's rep) organization superior to the competition in terms of product and category knowledge?
- Is the overall retail coverage factor (the number of stores the sales force calls on as a percentage of the total market universe) a strength compared to those of other major competitors in the industry?
- Does the size and breadth of the company's product line make the sales force exert more influence over a particular retail group versus the narrower focus of the principal competitors' product lines?

If after reviewing these guidelines you determine that, in fact, the company has superiority in one or more of the sales areas, the firm would be well advised to leverage that position to achieve a competitive advantage within the market and formulate future product development strategies that would capitalize upon that strength. In many cases, a firm may develop a parity product that, due to the power of its sales organization, can achieve market dominance or superior penetration at retail.

RESEARCH AND DEVELOPMENT

The research and development (R&D) function within a company is the source of future income flows, because that group is responsible for formulating, engineering, and developing the products that the company will bring to market. When the R&D function of a company is neglected, underdeveloped, or cut back due to budget constraints, it is often the precursor to the decline of the entity.

R&D, working in conjunction with the marketing and production departments of a company, usually provides the unique point of difference for the firm within the marketplace from a functional standpoint. It is then up to the marketing department to position the product preemptively, the production department to make the product economically, and the sales department to gain retail distribution of the product.

When evaluating the R&D function of a particular company for purposes of determining whether a competitive advantage exists, there is really only one critical question that must be answered in virtually every situation:

- Are the quality and integrity of the products within this company minimally at parity and preferably superior to those of the competition?

If the answer to this question is "no," the first step would be to achieve parity and then work towards achieving a superior product before entering competitive categories within a specific industry. If the answer to this question is "yes," then the company has a very powerful tool at its disposal, which is definitely a source for creating a competitive market advantage.

MARKETING

Determining whether or not a firm has a specific advantage in the area of marketing often helps to define the "rules of engagement" for waging competitive warfare. If the firm has a competitive advantage in the area of marketing, it may get by with being deficient in many other areas because of a strong ability to create consumer demand for its products.

There are countless numbers of cases involving companies whose sole source of leverage lay in their marketing ability (e.g., Reebok) and that was enough to catapult the firm to a market leadership position, often times covering up the deficiencies in other key functional areas. The relative strengths of the company can be evaluated vis-à-vis the following criteria:

- Does the company have dominant brands?
- Are there established "cash cows" (brands in the maturity phase of the product life cycle which generate large amounts of cash and require less marketing support)?
- Is the breadth of the product line sufficient to ensure a minimal amount of cannibalization?
- Is there a high degree of creativity in the company at present, and if not, are the resources available to secure creative input on a short-term basis?

While this is certainly not an exhaustive list of marketing criteria, it nevertheless covers the basic essentials a company needs to claim a specific advantage in the area of marketing.

9

THE CORPORATE LIFE CYCLE

Perhaps one of the most heavily utilized tools in the field of marketing is the product life cycle analysis, which was originated in the academic world over twenty-five years ago and today is still a very useful tool within the medicine bag of marketing executives. The product life cycle or PLC, analyzes where an individual brand or product stands along a time continuum, relating to the four key phases of a product's life:

- Introduction
- Growth
- Maturity
- Decline

Managers have utilized the PLC for years in order to determine the best marketing strategy to employ in growing the sales and/or profits of a particular brand or product. The PLC analysis requires that management of the brand take an honest look at the performance results and determine whether the brand is on the way up or on the way down.

While the task of analyzing where a specific product lies within the life cycle seems straightforward and obvious, it is in fact a very difficult exercise because it combines both quantitative and qualitative assessments. The latter can obviously be influenced (jaded) by the perspective, degree of ownership, and responsibility of the individual conducting the assessment. Therefore, while the task of determining whether a brand is still in its introductory phase (how long should that be?), in a growth phase (is that continuous growth or sporadic growth?), in a mature state (usually where volume is relatively flat over a twenty-four-month period or longer), or in the decline phase (where volume has dropped for at least twelve months and the prospects for a comeback in existing form seem slim to nonexistent) would seem to be rather straightforward, ''emotional analysis'' sometimes governs the process and can lead a management team astray.

To be successful, the product life cycle analysis should be a combined effort by those involved in the management of the entity. Once the brand's cycle position is accurately identified, the task of determining the proper strategy going forward becomes much easier.

One of the problems with the product life cycle analysis when utilized by senior management is that they must look at the total brand portfolio life cycle to get a true handle on what the overall corporate strategy should be. In a marketing-driven company with multiple brands/products, the resources of the firm are limited and the management team must determine which businesses merit investment spending and which business should be ''milked'' for cash to fuel the engine.

The latter concept is often referred to as the ''cash-cow''

strategy, whereby a mature brand with a good critical mass level would have its marketing support significantly reduced in order to generate a significant amount of cash. This strategy is usually employed when the firm believes that the brand is on the road to decline (in fact the cash-cow strategy may actually precipitate the decline phase) and that the money it could yield in a reduced-support state would yield a greater return if invested in another brand that is in the introductory or growth phase of its life cycle.

In order for the senior management team to accurately assess all of the brands in the company's portfolio and set the overall corporate strategy, they should ideally utilize another tool which takes the product life cycle to the corporate or divisional level. This tool is something I have called the corporate life cycle (CLC).

The CLC basically represents the accumulation of all the individual brand volume levels according to their particular phases of the PLC, and creates a snapshot view of where the company's volume breaks by introduction, growth, maturity, and decline. If four of the firm's ten brands are in the growth phase, for example, with combined sales totaling 30 percent of company-wide volume, then the firm can be said to have 30 percent of its businesses in a growth mode. Accordingly, the same exercise performed on the remaining brands in the company would yield a total picture of where the company stands today and what the prospects for future growth in sales and/or profitability can logically be.

The results of combining the individual brand PLCs into a CLC can be startling to members of senior management who have not used this type of tool before, because it keeps them from being lulled into the 3 to 5 percent growth game that many companies settle for in their annual budget process. Every firm goes through this 3 to 5 percent automatic growth when the annual budgets are being prepared and the logic of a modest growth rate is evaluated given the positive influences of price increases, inflation, expanded distribution, and the like. It is largely for this reason that companies miss their volume and profit targets on a regular basis.

The CLC is not a budgeting tool in and of itself, but it can be a most effective adjunct to the process of analyzing the current and future state of the business from a qualitative standpoint. The CLC can be used to help devise the overall growth strategy for the company, by determining what percentages of the company's volume should be in introduction, growth, maturity, and decline. It is important to note that the CLC can only work in this vein if the management of the firm understands the concept of managing products through the various phases of their life cycles.

If the management attempts to create a single business strategy that must then be employed across the board in every brand group, the results will often be very disappointing. The CLC is a macro tool that ultimately should be utilized by senior management in order to help the middle managers develop the micro-marketing strategies appropriate to their brands or products.

If the company were to set specific guidelines whereby 20 percent of the firm's volume should be in introduction, 40 percent in growth, 30 percent in maturity (yielding lots of cash), and 10 percent in decline, the individual brand strategies, new products and R&D programs, advertising and promotional programs, headcount requirements, and capital budgeting needs for the company would all come together. Obviously, if the company intends to have 20 percent of its volume in the introductory phase and 40 percent in the growth phase, a disproportionate amount of the advertising and promotional dollars must be allocated to those products. Further, the R&D budgets must reflect the manpower and machinery needs associated with creating enough products to generate 20 percent of the company's volume.

Many overzealous senior managers want 75 percent of the company's volume to be in the introductory and growth phases of the CLC, which is very expensive to manage and probably not the wisest move for creating a viable long-term business. Products in the introductory phase require heavy amounts of cash to support their initial efforts. They have achieved little or no visibility, are striving to gain retailer acceptance, and most consumers have never seen, heard of, or tried the product. In order to satisfy all of those needs, the firm must make significant investments in some or all of the following:

- Tooling
- Advertising production
- Media
- Sales discounts/allowances
- Incentive programs
- R&D testing
- Manpower

Accordingly, if the management of a firm stated their objective was to have 40 percent of their volume in the introductory phase, depending upon how many products that would consist of (one large one or three medium-size products), the cost to manage such a strategy would be substantial. Further, in order to preserve overall corporate profitability, the firm would have to have some "cash cows" on hand in order to fuel the cash needs of the introductory businesses. Absent the presence of cash-cow brands, the firm would probably have to report a loss or severe reduction in earnings, which could have a very detrimental effect on a highly leveraged private company or a public corporation.

Similarly, if the firm is too aggressive in its strategy for creating growth brands, which also require a significant amount of "fuel," the strategy can backfire, leaving the firm in a worse position than a moderate growth strategy would have yielded.

Time and again we read about companies that are on a negative profit growth binge, whereby the sales of the company are growing at such a rapid pace that the capital required to sustain the growth (advertising, promotion, manpower, inventory, working capital, warehousing, distribution systems, etc.) is in fact driving the firm into a significant loss position. In effect, the faster a firm like that grows, the deeper in trouble it gets.

This is often the case with companies in the high-tech and fashion industries, where an overnight success can occur, a product or line of products gets incredibly "hot," and the firm outgrows its managerial, financial, and operational capabilities. In retrospect, many such firms would have fared far better over the long term (and, in fact, would have lived to witness the long term) if the growth in sales had been managed towards the goal of maximizing profitability and asset utilization.

Therefore, the CLC should be used to help companies look at where they are today and as a tool to assess the needs of the business in order to drive it to the end goals stated in the long-term plan. The CLC can be a great governor of the planning process and also serve as a rather graphic pro-forma tool, which would enable senior management to accurately evaluate a number of "what if" scenarios resulting from the implementation of a high-growth, moderate-growth, low-growth, or no-growth strategy.

The real advantage of the CLC as a management tool is that members of the senior management team who are not in the marketing area can use it as a snapshot technique for evaluating the company's market position and to determine the proper resource management strategies to develop in support of the company's future goals.

10

THE CORPORATE
CAPABILITIES MATRIX

A major element in the engineering of a marketing turnaround is the creation of what I call a corporate capabilities matrix (CCM). The CCM analyzes current corporate technological capacity and its application to relevant product categories.

- It highlights products that can be developed quickly with minimal tooling and capital investment.

- It is the guiding light which will lead to increased plant and production efficiency while freeing up dollars for marketing investment.

- It helps to identify "quick strike" product opportunities while minimizing overall corporate financial exposure.

On the corporate capabilities matrix, the production capabilities of a plant are listed down the left hand side, and the potential categories that a firm could enter utilizing those production capacities across the top (see Table 4). The objective is to highlight for each particular production capacity element, which categories are currently represented by the company and to what degree they are represented. For example, if the firm produces a low-price shampoo but does not make a medium- or high-price shampoo, which could be produced on the same equipment, the production capabilities are not maximized.

After listing the categories the company has currently penetrated, a gap analysis will highlight the categories the company could enter right away with its existing production capacity even though it does not currently compete in those areas.

THE GAP ANALYSIS

The next step in utilizing the CCM is to conduct a "gap analysis," which helps to highlight the categories that provide a near-term (twelve to eighteen month) incremental business opportunity for the company, with very little capital expenditure required. The gap analysis uncovers the categories which the company does not currently compete in, but where the production capacity exists to enter quickly and cost efficiently.

Some examples of this at Fabergé USA during 1987–1988 were potential opportunities in the facial moisturizer, hand and body lotion, and suntan lotion business. Fabergé possessed filling equipment for shampoo and conditioners which could fill roughly 240 sixteen-ounce bottles per minute at a viscosity level of 11,000 centipoises (cps). Coincidentally, most hand and body lotion products come in 12- to 16-ounce bottles and range between 9,000 and 15,000 cps in viscosity (the higher the cps, the thicker the product). The same viscosity levels are found in the

TABLE 4

XYZ COMPANY
CORPORATE CAPABILITIES MATRIX

	Aerosol Filling	Liquid Process Filling	Solid Mass Filling	Oil/Water Filling
Deodorant				
Family	N	—	N	—
Men's	E/N	—	E/N	—
Women's	E/N	—	E/N	—
Anti-Perspirant				
Family	N	—	N	—
Men's	E/N	—	E/N	—
Women's	E/N	—	E/N	—
Hairspray				
Men's	N	N	—	—
Women's	E/N	E/N	—	—
Shaving Cream				
Men's	E/N	—	—	—
Women's	N	—	—	—
Shaving Gel				
Men's	N	—	—	—
Women's	N	—	—	—
Hair Mousse				
Men's	N	—	—	—
Women's	E/N	—	—	—
Room Fresheners	N	—	—	—
Shampoo				
Men's	—	E/N	—	—
Women's	—	E/N	—	—
Family	—	E/N	—	—
Conditioner				
Men's	—	E/N	—	—
Women's	—	E/N	—	—
Family	—	E/N	—	—
Hand & Body Lotion	—	N	—	—
Facial Moisturizer	—	N	—	—
Hair Gel				
Men's	—	N	—	—
Women's	—	E/N	—	—
Suntan Lotion	—	N	—	—
Suntan Oil	—	—	—	N
Lip Balm	—	—	N	—
Bar Soap	—	—	N	—
Liquid Soap	—	N	—	—
Fragrance	E/N	E/N	—	—

E = Existing Products   N = Potential for New Products

suntan lotion and facial moisturizing lotion categories, meaning that entry into those markets would be relatively easy for Fabergé if they were to do the following:

- Create a positioning for each product
- Develop the formula
- Design the packaging

Assuming those three tasks were completed according to the principles outlined in the "marketing turnaround blueprint," Fabergé USA could have begun marketing three totally new, incremental volume products on fully amortized equipment, yielding outstanding gross profit margins. In fact, the incremental volume produced on those products would help to increase the load factor of the plant, making the entire operation more profitable for the company.

In the case of Fabergé, this same scenario held true for the manufacturing of aerosol products. Fabergé's Aqua Net Aerosol, the world's largest hair spray brand, sold approximately 250 million cans per year and its Brut 33 deodorant and antiperspirant sprays sold another 30 to 40 million cans, so in total the company was producing almost 300 million aerosol cans per year. As a result, Fabergé invested heavily in aerosol filling equipment in order to become a low-cost producer and reap the substantial financial benefit of producing in-house.

The majority of Fabergé's competitors did not produce their own aerosol products and therefore could not compete (profitably) with the $.89 to $.99 retail price charged for nine-ounce Aqua Net Hairspray, the number-one selling item in the hair care industry. By definition, a company owning aerosol equipment would need to have multiple brands utilizing the technology or a major low price, high unit volume brand to make the vertical integration strategy work.

At Fabergé, a number of products were identified that could utilize the aerosol filling equipment:

1. Family deodorant/antiperspirant

2. Men's deodorant/antiperspirant

3. Women's deodorant/antiperspirant

4. Men's hair spray

5. Women's hair spray

6. Men's shaving cream

7. Men's shaving gel

8. Women's shaving cream

9. Hair mousse

10. Room deodorizer/air freshener

11. Insect repellent

12. First-aid spray

13. Window cleaner

14. Spray starch

15. Oven cleaner

16. Foot spray

17. Contact lens cleaner

Of the seventeen product categories listed, it was determined that numbers ten through seventeen did not fit within the mission of Fabergé as a personal care/beauty products company, but certainly all of the products listed from one through nine did fit in. In fact, the company was currently involved in several of those categories in a minor way. What was needed was a major commitment to developing higher volume products in those areas consistent with the image of Fabergé.

Similar exercises were conducted for the areas of solid mass filling, liquid process filling, and oil/water filling, and were extended to the extrusion and injection molding areas for packaging components. These exercises proved to be enormously successful for the company and helped to direct the entire new product effort from the manufacturing facility up—a radical approach in today's marketing world.

This process can be applied to virtually any manufacturing business for purposes of generating new products or line extensions, and for utilizing excess capacity (which can cripple a P&L statement) to subcontract fill products for other manufacturers.

Ultimately, understanding the financial rewards of increasing production efficiency impacts the areas of marketing, design, R&D, and operations and truly helps to make the organization work as a team, collectively committed to maximizing volume and profit. The next chapter presents further details about Fabergé's marketing turnaround.

11

FABERGÉ USA, INC.

In December 1986 Fabergé USA, Inc. had become known as a tired manufacturer of personal care, beauty care, and fragrance products sold in the food, drug, and mass merchandiser classes of trade. At one point back in the late 1960s and early 1970s, Fabergé had been known as a marketer of high quality fragrance products; the Brut brand, with legendary spokesman Joe Namath, was one of the most successful fragrance brands ever introduced.

By 1986 little of that imagery remained. Fabergé was becoming well known for selling some of the most inexpensive, heavily discounted products in the market and subscribing to what many referred to as the ''stack 'em high, watch 'em fly'' strategy of marketing. In fact, Fabergé was doing very little marketing and was instead driving the business solely on the basis of price. This was a dangerous strategy in a market with competitors such as Procter & Gamble, Gillette, Lever Brothers, Clairol, and Revlon, to name but a few. Fabergé, though still profitable, had little prospect for future growth due to the aging, tired nature of its products and the already depressed pricing structure it operated under.

The key element at Fabergé that enabled it to become a very profitable, truly dynamic company was the existence of one of the most efficient, vertically integrated manufacturing facilities in the entire consumer products industry. The Fabergé manufacturing facility, located in Raeford, North Carolina, had the ability to produce huge numbers of aerosol, solid, and liquid filled products at very favorable cost levels compared to its competitors in the industry. In fact, the Fabergé manufacturing facility and its stable of products created the impression that the company was "shooting a fly with a cannon."

Accordingly, upon joining the company, one of the first things I did was attempt to review the marketing plans and positions of each of the major brands and to gain an understanding of the depth and breadth of Fabergé's manufacturing capability within the personal care, beauty care, and fragrance categories. The major brands within Fabergé as of December 1986 were as follows:

- Brut Cologne
- Brut 33 Toiletries (deodorant, anti-perspirant, etc.)
- Aqua Net Hairspray
- Aqua Net Silk Protein Shampoo, Conditioner, Hair Care
- Fabergé Organics Shampoo and Conditioner
- Babe Cologne and Toiletries
- Just Wonderful Hairspray
- Tigress Cologne

Aqua Net maintained a leadership position within the aerosol hair spray market, with approximately a 30 percent share, but had difficulty securing a meaningful share within the non-aerosol segment. The Aqua Net Silk Protein line of hair care products made up less than 1 percent of the hair care market and looked like they were heading for oblivion, even with celebrity spokeswoman Donna Mills.

The Brut fragrance brand was a shadow of its former self, having dwindled to the point of questionable viability within the men's fragrance market, while its line extension, Brut 33 Toiletries (so named because the products contained 33 percent of the fragrance level found in Brut Cologne) was one of the leading men's toiletries brands in the United States, with the number-two position within the aerosol deodorant/antiperspirant market and the number-three position within the men's stick segment.

Fabergé Organics Shampoo and Conditioner was a throwback to the flower-children, psychedelic 1970s, with a thick, viscous, wheat germ oil and honey formula and packaging that featured wild colored, non flip-top caps. The brand competed solely on the basis of price and only sold well at retail when featured at $.99. The S. C. Johnson company introduced a brand during the mid-1980s called Hälsa, which was an updated version of Fabergé Organics, and the brand was effectively eroding the Organics user base with their more contemporary products.

Babe was yet another throwback brand, having achieved most of its success back in the early 1970s with then-spokeswoman Margaux Hemingway as the "Babe Girl." The Babe fragrance was virtually dead in the market and the Babe Toiletries line was an attempt by Fabergé to create the female equivalent of the Brut 33 men's toiletries line. The strategy was somewhat successful as the toiletries business began to dwarf the almost nonexistent fragrance business, but the continued vitality of this dated looking brand was severely in question.

Just Wonderful Hairspray was just that—back in the 1950s and 60s when it was one of the top brands in the market. However the brand went the way of the beehive hairdo and had dwindled to minor brand status by the 1980s. The package graphics were virtually identical to those utilized some twenty-five years earlier and the Fabergé name did not appear on the label. Instead, the name Carol Richards appeared (I believe those were the names of the former owner's children). Were it not for the fact that Fabergé owned and operated its own aerosol manufacturing facility, the Just Wonderful Hairspray brand would have died a long time ago. In fact, the brand's claim to fame in the 1980s was its inclusion in the movie *Hairspray,* a spoof on the 1950s hairstyles, a low budget film released to movie theaters during 1987.

Tigress Cologne was at one time a "hot" fragrance brand. Lola Falana was its Tigress Woman in the 1970s, dressed in a leopard outfit and crawling provocatively across the TV screen. By 1986 the Tigress brand had virtually disappeared from the market and Fabergé had no plans to revive the line.

By the mid-1980s, therefore, Fabergé was a company with an upscale image as a marketer of fine fragrance and beauty products (largely a holdover from its past and perhaps a result of its association in people's minds with the precious Fabergé eggs). In fact, Fabergé was a low-cost manufacturer of inexpensive personal care items, with dated imagery, sold at heavily discounted retail prices. If ever there was a firm that was the perfect candidate for a marketing turnaround it was Fabergé.

One of the great downfalls of most manufacturing companies is their inability to move a sufficient number of units through their plant(s) to cover all of the fixed costs of the facility. Many times firms in this predicament develop new products that require significant amounts of new tooling and/or need to be manufactured outside the company due to technological limitations. In this situation, a company may simply be exacerbating the problem because the new product volume/profit is not nearly sufficient to offset the negative manufacturing variances effected by an underutilized manufacturing facility.

In creating the corporate capabilities matrix for Fabergé it became very clear that the company's key tangible asset was its manufacturing facility, and the key intangible asset was the name Fabergé. Because of the breadth of the Fabergé name awareness and the multiplicity of product categories within the personal care/beauty care arena which the firm did not presently compete in, the prospect for introducing new, noncannibalistic products with exceptionally favorable cost of goods levels and relatively short payback periods was exceptionally strong.

Therefore, after creating a CCM for the company, we began to prioritize which product categories to pursue first in order to satisfy the following key objectives:

- Help solidify the existing Aqua Net, Brut, Brut 33, Fabergé Organics, and Just Wonderful brands.
- Provide incremental, highly profitable volume within the men's and women's personal care markets.
- Create Fabergé market/category dominance by combining both existing and new products.
- Have products fully developed and ready to go to market within twelve months of the completion of the CCM analysis.

The following categories were of utmost importance in realizing the aforementioned objectives:

- Non-aerosol hair spray
- Men's stick deodorant/antiperspirant
- Men's fragrance

- Men's aerosol deodorant/antiperspirant
- Women's hair care (gel, mousse, shampoo, conditioner)
- Men's shaving cream

A segmentation analysis of the appropriate markets was constructed to pinpoint need gaps and to help properly position the new entries that would ultimately be developed. In addition, this analysis helped to indicate whether the proper strategy was to develop the products as line-extensions of existing brands or to develop entirely new brand names for the entries. The analysis showed that there was significant upside potential within the existing brand names for line-extensions, and that in some cases the firm could enter a single market with both a line-extension and a totally new brand at different price points to penetrate different subsegments within the market.

The team then went back to the product category priority list (developed through an analysis of the CCM) and began to attach brand names, product positionings, and price-points to the anticipated new entries. A number of potential brand names were developed and tested among potential target customers. This ultimately led to the development of new product formulas and packaging through a combination of in-house and outside talent.

In addition to the segmentation analyses, creative sessions, and market research, the team held a series of risk assessment meetings, in an attempt to determine the real financial risks associated with each of the new entries. Specifically, if a new item did not require new tooling, would help to recover a significant amount of manufacturing overhead, and had a very low chance of cannibalizing the existing brands, the "risk" of introducing the product was considered acceptable. Initial inventory exposure had to be carefully managed against trade commitments and early consumer sell-through reports.

This type of "gauge and go" decision making is especially useful in turnaround situations involving an aging asset with a vulnerable core and a relatively high fixed overhead base. Large conglomerates, such as Procter & Gamble or Gillette would not subscribe to this type of system, but they do not face the same types of pressures encountered by a firm like Fabergé. The encumbrances of some large corporate environments highlight some of the exciting opportunities which exist when the senior management of smaller, entrepreneurial companies have the benefit of big company experience to aid their firm while running at a high rate of speed. In those instances, the executive (entrepreneur) knows the limitation of their larger, more formal competitors and can utilize that knowledge along with an expeditious tool like the CCM to beat the larger competitor to market.

After conducting the "gauge and go" sessions and reassessing its CCM priority list, Fabergé's team moved ahead and developed more than ten new products in a very short time frame. Six of those were brought to market within twelve months of conducting the initial CCM analysis. Some of the new products or line-extensions developed and introduced during the marketing turnaround period were:

- Fabergé Organics Shampoo and Conditioner (relaunched)
- Cut Guard Shaving Cream (introduced)
- McGregor Cologne for Men (introduced)
- Aqua Net Non-Aerosol Hairspray (relaunched)
- Aqua Net Silk Protein Haircare Line (relaunched)
- Just Wonderful Hairspray (relaunched)
- Just Wonderful Shampoo and Conditioner (introduced)
- Tenax Haircare Line (introduced)
- Extra-Strength Brut 33 Deodorant/Anti-Perspirant (introduced)

- Brut 33 Shaving Cream (relaunched)
- Fabergé European Salon Formula Haircare Line (introduced)

These products involved completely redesigned packaging graphics and containers, improved or entirely new formulations, and completely revised marketing platforms. Fabergé increased its volume from approximately $230 million in 1986 to over $400 million in 1988, and was earning in excess of $50 million in profit, a whopping 12.5 percent of sales (versus an industry average of 6 to 8 percent). This was judged to be one of the most successful marketing turnarounds in many years in the consumer products industry and helped to make Fabergé a formidable, highly respected player within its various markets.

In addition, the development of the CCM helped us at Fabergé create a new brand of stick deodorant and antiperspirant for men called Power Stick. The brand was introduced in late 1988 and today is considered one of the largest, most successful men's toiletries introductions of the 1980s. In a rare move, Fabergé invested heavily in new filling and packaging tooling for Power Stick in the belief that it might be a $100 million product. Furthermore, it was necessary to make a preemptive design statement in a crowded, very brand-loyal category.

However, to stay true to the credo of making tools go as far as possible, the turnaround team decided to take all of the Fabergé stick deodorant/antiperspirant products and put them in this newly designed container. That decision not only improved the aesthetics of all of the other sticks, which had been in stock supplier containers, but it also helped achieve the following:

- Faster amortization of the Power Stick tooling because it was used for several million additional units of Brut, Brut 33, and Extra Strength Brut 33 products.

- The sophisticated nature of the new Power Stick tools meant that all sticks could be run on faster, fully automated filling equipment, which yielded significant savings in cost of goods.

- Aesthetically, the new containers appeared much larger on a two-and-one-half ounce product, thus dramatically improving the shelf presence and competitive visual position versus other major men's brands.

Power Stick was the first mega-launch from Fabergé in over fifteen years and was the subject of many heated internal debates, but in the end it was a tremendous move for the firm and clearly solidified its position as the leader in the men's stick deodorant market, something it could not claim just three years earlier.

Fabergé acquired Elizabeth Arden from Eli Lilly, Inc. for $725 million in 1988, thus making Fabergé a firm doing roughly $1 billion from a mere $230 million in 1986. In early 1989, Fabergé was sold to Unilever, N.V. for a reported $1.6 billion, netting the owners of Fabergé a profit of several hundred million dollars from the sale of the business. Not bad for a firm that had been referred to as a sleepy, budget-product manufacturer just three years earlier.

12

VALUE ENGINEERING

When faced with the daunting task of having to conduct a corporate or marketing turnaround, the hardest thing for a management team to do is to find ways to quickly increase the company's cash flow and create a lasting change that will not adversely impact the business.

Several so-called turnaround artists institute cost-cutting programs that can best be described as "stripping measures," many times sacrificing the quality of the product and/ or the operation of the business. While some of these measures may be justified in the face of an impending "meltdown" situation, often they are the result of an overzealous turnaround team searching for the quick fix to a very complex problem.

The concept of "value engineering," in contrast, involves a thorough evaluation and analysis of the company's product lines and production processes and finding ways to perform the functions or create the products more economically without sacrificing the overall perceived quality level in the eyes of the consumer or end user. Many companies perform some level of value engineering on an ongoing basis, but it is usually within the domain of a lower- or middle-level manager, who does not have the full support of senior management.

A new senior manager may come into a company and suggest a new way of building a certain product and may discover that a lower-level manager had submitted a similar idea months earlier, only to be rebuffed by a superior who was not interested in making the same product for less money. A wise move for any new management or turnaround team is to seek out those individuals involved in the value engineering/value analysis function, in order to fully analyze and understand any programs that have been developed in the past and either accepted or rejected. Many times ideas have been rejected not because they are not good, but because the general modus operandi of the company does not place a premium on this type of work.

There is no more important task in a company than constantly reevaluating the manufacturing and design process to determine how to build "a better mousetrap" (or at least one that is just as good) for less cost than the firm is paying today. The concept of utilizing the funds generated from the successful value engineering of a product line to create a more aggressive advertising or promotional campaign on an undersupported product line is one of the central tenets of the entire marketing turnaround blueprint.

The previously discussed corporate capabilities matrix (CCM) is not only a tool for uncovering the breadth of the various manufacturing capacities within a given company, but it can also be used as a vehicle to stimulate the value engineering process. The development of a major restaging/repositioning of a shampoo and conditioner product line from a leading beauty products company provides a good example of how value engineering can be absolutely invaluable in creating a marketing "war chest." We will call the product Brand X from Company XYZ.

Company XYZ had been marketing a shampoo and conditioner product line under the name Brand X for almost twenty years, using essentially the same packaging, positioning, and formulation during that entire period. Unfortunately for both the company and the brand, the shampoo/conditioner market changed dramatically during that time and Brand X went from being one of the top brands in the entire market to an also-ran that did not even rank within the top twenty brands in the market some two decades later.

The decline of Brand X was rather slow throughout the 1977–1985 period, when its positioning in the marketplace was still unique (or unencroached) and consumers still saw a validity in the message the brand had to deliver. Then, in 1985, a major competitor launched a 1980s version of the dated Brand X positioning and virtually destroyed the consumer franchise for Brand X within a 15-month period. The major question facing the XYZ Company, owner of Brand X, was whether to turn it into a total price-value brand and compete solely on the basis of low price, or to reposition the brand and develop it into a formidable competitor once again. The decision was made to adopt the latter strategy and reposition the brand as an updated product line addressing the needs of the hair care consumer today.

In conducting an objective analysis of Brand X and its demise within the market, a list of the top ten brands in the hair care market was compiled. For each brand, elements such as price, positioning, promotion, packaging, formulation, line extension, advertising, and manufacturing process were evaluated and a determination of effectiveness was attached to each brand. The analysis concluded that Brand X was deficient in three critical areas:

- Positioning
- Formulation
- Packaging

This was not meant to imply that the other areas mentioned in the evaluative checklist were all performing in a stellar manner, but it was deemed critical to modify and improve the positioning, formulation, and packaging of Brand X if it were to try once again to occupy a unique competitive niche within the hair care market.

In evaluating the three key variables listed above in terms of the competitive framework of the hair care market, a CCM analysis had been utilized to help determine how to reduce costs and maximize product efficacy, filling speed, and a variety of other variables versus the known attributes of other major product lines in the marketplace. Specifically, it was determined that Brand X was positioned as a throwback to the 1970s, because its formula did not address the key consumer hot buttons of the late 1980s:

- Body and shine
- Rinsability
- Conditioning properties

The product was engineered with a thick, viscous formula that created a low level of rinsability and, in fact, discouraged consumers who used the shampoo from using the conditioner. Because the thick formula left a residue in the hair, giving it an oily look and feel with prolonged use, this obviated the need to use a conditioner, whose principal function is to give hair a smooth shiny look and feel. Since conditioners also tend to leave an oily buildup over time, women with naturally oily hair rarely use them.

Therefore, Brand X was actually working against itself in many ways: the formula did not rinse well, leaving the consumer with an oily scalp, which prevented her from wanting to use the Brand X (or any other) conditioning product. In addition, the packaging of the product did not feature the flip-top caps that were so prevalent in the market during 1986. Instead the brand used the big, old-fashioned screw-off caps, allowing water to enter the bottle in the shower and creating a less efficacious product for the consumer after just a few uses.

Another packaging disadvantage was that the bottles were screened with old-fashioned Brand X logos and they were transparent. This had the double negative effect: It showed the consumer the thick, viscous formula amidst an array of thinner formulations, and it also required the XYZ Company to overfill the fifteen-ounce bottles to sixteen ounces, because of something called an aesthetic fill. In laymen's terms, this means that the XYZ Company was putting one extra ounce in each standard fifteen-ounce bottle to avoid giving the appearance of a bottle that had been used or underfilled. At a cost of six cents per ounce on production of forty million bottles per year, the aesthetic fill feature necessitated by the transparent polypropylene bottle was costing the XYZ Company something on the order of $2.4 million per year!

Brand X was thus plagued by a number of problems, which severely hindered its competitive position in the market and potentially cost the XYZ Company valuable dollars in the manufacturing process:

- Formula was too viscous, measuring 10,000 cps versus the category average of 2,500 cps.
- The viscous formula was not only hurting rinsability but was also slowing down the filling process to 160 bottles per minute, versus the category average of 290 bottles per minute on the exact same equipment.

- The transparent polypropylene bottles were costing the XYZ Company four cents per bottle more than an opaque high-density polyethylene bottle would cost (like the rest of the category was using), which on a 40 million unit volume base amounted to a potential cost savings of $1.6 million.

- The see-through nature of the polypropylene bottles versus the opaque high-density polyethylene bottles was costing the firm $2.4 million in free ounces due to the aesthetic fill attribute of see-through bottles on Brand X.

- The packaging graphics were much harder to apply on the transparent bottles versus the opaque bottles, because the transparent bottles showed all the "sins," where the rejection level would be much lower on an opaque unit.

- The older, screw-off cap was not only causing the consumer to dilute the formula (rendering it ineffective), but it was making her use less product per shampooing. A flip-top cap, although it would normally cost more, was actually the same cost as the older cap because it was much smaller in size. Further, the orifice could be built so that it would dispense the desired amount of product (by the manufacturer, XYZ), thereby enhancing both the use-up rate and the viability of the entire contents of the bottle.

The marketing group looked at the situation and decided to reposition Brand X as a more contemporary product, with a state-of-the-art formula and contemporary packaging. They planned to utilize the value engineering of the restaged product (the savings) to fund the relaunch in the first year and to capture the savings as profit in year two and beyond. It was felt that in order to support the repositioned product in the highly competitive price-value segment of the shampoo/conditioner market, a marketing spending level of $8 million was needed to help generate $30 million in net sales. Given the financial situation at the XYZ Company, incremental funding for the restage was not an option, so that the money had to come from the value engineering process itself.

The good news is that the $8 million did come from the value engineering process, broken down as follows:

- $2.4 million from elimination of aesthetic fill
- $1.6 million from move to high-density polyethylene bottles
- $1.6 million from reduction in fill time (viscosity)
- $0.8 million from savings in ingredients (viscosity)
- $0.4 million from lower screening rejection rate
- $0.8 million from auto-torquing of flip-top caps
- $0.6 million from moving to a single common cap for all bottles

These value engineering elements provided the XYZ Company with a dynamic looking product line (the new Brand X) and armed it with an $8.2 million dollar war chest, in addition to the $7 million dollars the brand was already spending on advertising and promotion in its former existence. Accordingly, Brand X was relaunched with a huge $15.2 million blitz that not only helped to resuscitate this languishing product line, but helped to drive the brand into the top ten within the hair care market and yield significantly increased profits in year two and beyond.

The value engineering process, through the analytical advantages of the corporate capabilities matrix, helped the XYZ Company to zero in on its cost of goods deficiencies. In conjunction with a well thought out marketing strategy, the process helped to yield a repositioned brand that was more profitable, better looking, more efficacious, and longer lived.

Value engineering can be performed most effectively when it is put into the following twelve-step process, which should serve as a value engineering checklist for the turnaround team (see also Figure 4):

1. Evaluate all primary packaging materials to determine if cost of the product can be reduced without sacrificing aesthetics or functional characteristics.

2. Evaluate the manufacturing process to determine how to maximize speed of assembly, filling, etc.

3. Evaluate all of the ingredients of the product to determine the cost/efficacy trade-off.

4. Evaluate the number of steps required to create the product and whether the materials, formulation, packaging, etc. can be better utilized in a more synchronous manner.

5. Vertically integrate the manufacturing components wherever critical mass exists in order to minimize subcontracting fees and further capture efficiencies within the burden rate of the company's manufacturing facility (e.g., blow mold your own bottles, screen your own logos, etc.).

6. Find multiple uses for existing manufacturing equipment in order to accelerate the depreciation/amortization schedule of the tooling and yield a more favorable overall cost of goods rate on a faster timetable.

7. Analyze ways in which the company can leverage its manufacturing strengths to benefit products in seemingly unrelated categories.

8. Make investments in equipment that will lower the labor component of the plant and effect a lower defect rate.

9. Ensure that all product features are providing value to the ultimate consumer where a more economical

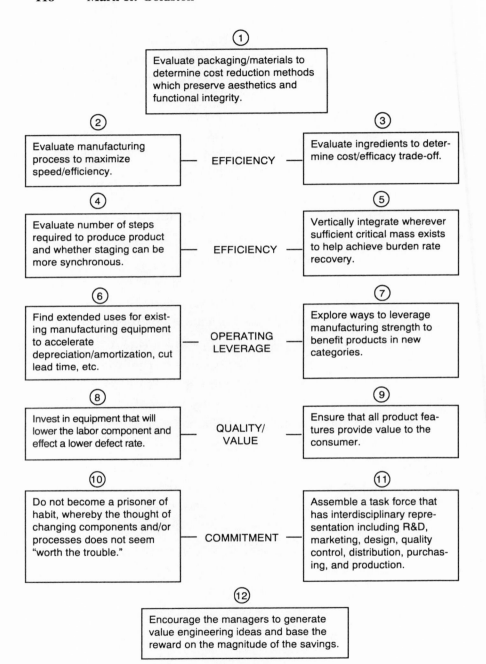

FIGURE 4

THE TWELVE-STEP VALUE ENGINEERING FORECAST

alternative exists that does not significantly reduce the overall aesthetic or efficacy properties of the product.

10. Do not become a prisoner of habit, whereby the thought of changing components and/or processes does not seem "worth the trouble."

11. Ensure that a value engineering task force is assembled that features interdisciplinary representation and always includes members from the manufacturing, marketing, R&D, design, quality control, distribution/shipping, and purchasing departments.

12. Encourage the managers of the company to generate value engineering ideas and base the reward on the magnitude of the savings.

Applying the twelve-step value engineering checklist to any manufacturing company or any other company that utilizes a high degree of subcontracted manufacturing in a limited number of facilities can yield incredible savings over the long term. The value engineering process is critical to the turnaround team and, when used in conjunction with the corporate capabilities matrix, dramatic results can be achieved within one to two years that will last well into the future.

13

PRODUCT POSITIONING: THE MARKETING BIRTH CERTIFICATE

A product positioning statement is the "birth certificate" of a particular product. Positioning refers to the unique set of characteristics associated with a particular product. The positioning of the product should help to clarify what the product is, what it is to be used for, and by whom the product will be used. Positioning can mean the difference between life and death for a product because it sets up expectation criteria for consumers which they will use in two ways:

1. To determine whether to buy the product

2. To determine how the product worked versus what it promised at the time of purchase

Additionally, the product positioning statement should feature
the following (see also Figure 5):

1. A distinct reason for being for the product
2. A clear statement of who should use the product and
    what specifically the product is designed to do
3. A message that is easily understood upon examination of
    the package without the benefit of having seen the ad-
    vertising
4. Some characteristic of the product that would induce
    users of competitive products to switch

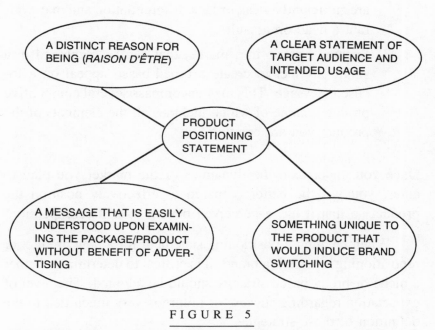

FIGURE 5

THE FOUR KEY ELEMENTS OF A PRODUCT POSITIONING
STATEMENT

WHAT ROLE DOES SEGMENTATION PLAY?

A thorough, well-conceived segmentation analysis is critical to creating a unique, focused product positioning statement. Without the segmentation analysis of the specific category the firm intends to enter, it would be virtually impossible to create a well-focused, preemptive positioning for a product. Later in this text there is a section entitled "Creating and Utilizing a Market Segmentation Analysis" which details the process used in creating effective, focused segmentation studies. These analyses help to highlight gaps in the market which can be defined in three ways:

1. Areas of the market in which there are no products positioned against specific performance/image criteria, referred to as "niches."
2. Areas of the market in which the "incumbent" brands are sufficiently weak or lack differentiation and may warrant a head-on assault.
3. Specific criteria in a market that can be combined in a single product to create a broad-based appeal on a focused message. This may encompass several competitive products, none of which includes all the elements of the product you are creating.

Once you understand the dynamics of the market you plan to enter, you will be better prepared to effectively position the product so that it has a perceived benefit over its competition.

When creating a positioning statement for a new product or repositioning an existing brand, it is critical to determine whether a niche or broad-based strategy should be adopted. The level of expectation regarding success or failure is very much tied to the definition of those strategies.

Successful products today can be traced back to effective niche strategies, which allowed them to enter a market they eventually dominated because of their ability to draw the masses into the niche (thus expanding that niche into a broad base). A good example of this phenomenon is the Tylenol brand analgesic by McNeil Consumer Products, a division of Johnson & Johnson.

THE TYLENOL PHENOMENON

Back in the early 1970s, Tylenol analgesic was a prescription product available only in pharmacies, designed and prescribed for those individuals who experienced upset stomach, gastrointestinal bleeding, or had ulcer-related problems. The product was effective in relieving pain and reducing fever, but was not effective as a blood thinner or in reducing swelling, both of which were characteristics of aspirin-based products. Accordingly, Tylenol was a specialty product with sales of approximately $50 million, while brands such as Bayer and Anacin were general, over-the-counter aspirin-based analgesics, with sales in the $250–500 million range.

Interestingly, an industrious group of McNeil marketing and R&D executives started conducting tests which showed that many people who did not suffer from the adverse side effects of aspirin-based products felt it was a good idea to take Tylenol anyway because it sounded as if it were safer and just as effective as aspirin. This became the new marketing strategy for the Tylenol business and by the mid-1970s the brand was readily available over the counter and registered sales in excess of $100 million.

Then, in 1976, McNeil introduced Extra-Strength Tylenol, which contained 500 mg. of acetaminophen (the sole ingredient in Tylenol) versus the 325 mg. level in regular strength Tylenol. Further, tests showed that for relief of pain and reduction of fever, Extra-Strength Tylenol was just as effective as a regular strength version of aspirin. Eureka! Why should anyone buy aspirin when Extra-Strength Tylenol was safer than aspirin and just as effective? The introduction of Extra-Strength Tylenol rocketed the total Tylenol franchise to over $500 million by 1980; today the total sales of Tylenol analgesic products approach $800 million, including Tylenol Cold Formula, Tylenol Sinus Medication, and Children's Tylenol.

Tylenol is a classic example of taking a niche product and changing the landscape of a category so that the niche becomes the dominant element and the appeal becomes broad-based. In fact, the expansion of the appeal of acetaminophen (Tylenol) as a general analgesic for everyone created a niche gap in the analgesic market. Accordingly, firms such as Bristol-Myers and American Home Products introduced Nuprin and Advil, respectively, over-the-counter ibuprofen products containing milder doses of the active ingredient found in the prescription pain-reliever, Motrin. These products were marketed strictly for pain relief and as such had a great appeal to arthritics and individuals with sports injuries. Tylenol (and acetaminophen products) migrated from niche status to broad-base status, leaving an opportunity for a new niche to develop which was seized by Nuprin and Advil. Not surprisingly, in order to reduce McNeil's vulnerability to another non-aspirin based analgesic/pain reliever (like Nuprin and Advil) taking away valuable aspirin converts, McNeil introduced Medipren in 1987, an ibuprofen product identical to Nuprin and Advil, under the tag line "when you haven't got time for the pain."

PROCTER & GAMBLE'S PERT SHAMPOO: IF AT FIRST YOU DON'T SUCCEED . . .

Whereas in the Tylenol example, McNeil took a very effective, limited appeal niche product and redefined the analgesic market in order to transform acetaminophen-based analgesics into mainstream products, the Procter & Gamble Pert Shampoo story is totally different.

In February 1979, Cincinnati, Ohio-based marketing powerhouse P&G introduced a shampoo called "Pert" into test market. The product was packaged in a bright green (almost chartreuse) bottle, with a multicolored label that was strangely similar to P&G's hot-selling deodorant soap, Coast. The product was judged "successful" in test (what "successful" meant P&G wouldn't say) and in 1980, Pert Shampoo was launched nationally with the advertising slogan "For bouncin' and behavin' hair."

Try as they might, P&G could not make a success out of Pert Shampoo during the 1980–1984 period. A failed test market in Milwaukee, Wisconsin, of Pert Creme Rinse and Conditioner from July 1980 to April 1982 did nothing to help Pert's future prospects. It was not as if P&G was treading unfamiliar water. Their Head & Shoulders Dandruff Shampoo was the number one brand in the total shampoo market (not just the dandruff market) and for years their Prell brand maintained a formidable presence among the top five to seven brands in the market. However, with Pert Shampoo something was clearly not right. It could have been the not-so-desirable similarity of the packaging to the male-based Coast deodorant soap. It could have been the bright, gaudy, noncosmetic image of the chartreuse packaging, the short, squat nature of the bottle, or the "soapy" fragrance of the product. Whatever it was, in November 1984, P&G reintroduced Pert Shampoo with new sleeker packaging, in a more muted shade of green, with a modified logo and more pleasant scent. The result: unsuccessful!

P&G could have packed it in and said that Pert was just another tombstone in the new-product cemetery of consumer package goods. They could have done that, but it would have been inconsistent with their corporate policy of "stick-with-it-until-it-works," no matter how long it may take. A company the size of P&G can afford to have that kind of attitude, because the success or failure of one product is not going to materially affect earnings per share.

So P&G borrowed a page from the shampoo market history book. They must have looked back at 1970 and seen that the number-one shampoo in the market then was Protein 21 by Mennen. The unique feature of Protein 21 was that it combined shampoo and conditioner in one product. The brand had quickly gained a 13 percent share of the market and was at the top of a very competitive heap. Had Mennen not fallen into the classic line-extension trap of taking the Protein 21 name and putting it on everything, including a separate conditioner product (thus defeating the combination product positioning) and a men's line called Protein 29 (immediately signaling to existing male users of Protein 21 that they were using a "women's" product), they might still today have a dominant hair care brand, instead of less than a one percent share of the market.

P&G took the original Protein 21 concept and created "Pert Plus," a shampoo and conditioner in one product. Introduced into test market with smashing results in Seattle, Washington, during 1985, Pert Plus was introduced nationally in November 1986 under the positioning line: "100% shampoo and 100% conditioner in one product. Eliminates the need for a separate conditioner." (Sound familiar, Protein 21 fans?)

We must give credit to Procter & Gamble for creating this positioning for Pert Plus and for taking a brand name (Pert) that had failed several times over a seven-year period (1979–1986) and not only reviving it beyond the 2 percent share it held prior to restage, but rocketing the brand to a 6 percent share of market in a fifteen-month period and placing it in the top two or three brands in the shampoo market today.

Pert Plus is clearly a niche product. However, instead of taking a niche product and adopting a specialty focus (as McNeil did originally with Tylenol), P&G used the primary feature of two-in-one (or two for the price of one) to create a mid-priced product that had two critical consumer advantages: convenience and high perceived value.

This is a classic example of conducting a marketing turnaround on a brand in a "war-zone" category that would not take kindly to any new "me-too" entrant, least of all one carrying a name that had failed several times before. The niche carved out by P&G with Pert Plus is the result of a sound segmentation analysis and pinpoint positioning, utilizing trigger elements like convenience and value that are relevant to the majority of purchasers in the hair care category.

Minnetonka Corporation: "Soft Soap" and "Check-Up"—Two Guppies That Got Swallowed by Whales

There are several instances where the creation of innovative niche products by smaller manufacturers with limited resources leads to the creation of huge subsegments of major markets at the expense of the innovative pioneer. The classic example of this phenomenon striking on not one but two occasions is the story of Minnetonka Corporation.

The Soft Soap Saga

Based in Minnetonka, Minnesota, the Minnetonka Corporation created a product in 1977 called "Soft Soap," which was liquid hand/facial soap sold in a plastic pump dispenser bottle. Consumers who were accustomed to bar soap for personal cleansing and liquid (detergent) soap for dishes and household cleaning found the concept difficult to grasp. The mere sound of the description "liquid soap" had an industrial ring to it.

Minnetonka created a niche by combining the unique product form (liquid) with a packaging innovation using screened patterns (wicker, bamboo, flowers, etc.) on the plastic dispensers. These made ideal displays in guest bathrooms, where the sight of a partially used bar of soap would mar an otherwise perfect, crisp setting. Clearly, Minnetonka viewed Soft Soap as a specialty product and did little or no advertising, making no reference to the benefits of using a liquid soap versus a bar soap. Interestingly, the medical profession has been using liquid soaps to "scrub" before surgery for years, but this angle never crept into the Soft Soap message. Soft Soap was as likely to be sold with the home novelty items as an accessory (like bathbeads) as much as it was sold as a conventional soap.

Well, it didn't take long for the message to reach Procter & Gamble and the other major bar soap manufacturers. What should they do? Wait for this upstart nuisance to go away, or create a liquid soap of their own? Clearly, there were huge financial considerations involved, given that P&G and the others had major dollar investments in highly efficient, low cost of goods bar soap machinery and were not eager to compete with themselves using plastic containers, pumps, and other elements that would reduce their return on invested capital.

On the other hand, how long could the major soap manufacturers sit and wait while Soft Soap secured an unchallenged position in their market? Most major soap manufacturers decided to bite the bullet and create liquid soap line extensions to brands like Ivory and Dial, pummeling poor little Minnetonka and their Soft Soap brand. The line was eventually sold to Colgate in 1988 for approximately $60 million, but it remains nevertheless a classic example of a small company that carves out a niche which ultimately leads to a huge market that they can no longer compete in (but here is $60 million for your trouble).

Time for a "Check-Up"

Another innovative product from Minnetonka was "Check-Up" toothpaste, the first product to claim that it actually helped to fight plaque buildup, the number-one cause of tooth decay and gum disease. Check-Up was truly an innovative product and just as in the case of Soft Soap, Minnetonka utilized a unique pump dispenser that stood up on the shelf, with a push button on top to dispense a "dose" of the product onto the toothbrush.

Check-Up was advertised as the first toothpaste designed to fight plaque, which was the buzzword in the oral care category and the subject of numerous articles on gum disease. Check-Up focused on plaque and tartar buildup, and this led to a host of new mouth rinse products by other manufacturers which helped to fight plaque.

Does the story begin to sound familiar? The big guys, P&G, Colgate, and Lever Brothers, attacked with a vengeance, introducing "Tartar Control" Crest, Colgate, and "Extra Strength" Aim—three new line extensions from the dominant players in the toothpaste market in response to the ripple created on the pond by Minnetonka's Check-Up. Not only did the Big Three introduce tartar control formulas, but they spent significantly on advertising, making it sound as if they had been perfecting the product for years. They also offered new, stand-up pump dispensers identical to the one used for Check-Up.

Once again David had shown Goliath the playing field only to have his ball taken away. Minnetonka and Check-Up gave birth to a massive new segment of the toothpaste market and then had a hard time getting invited to their own party. As in the case of Soft Soap, the brand (which was also line-extended into a Check-Up plaque-fighting gum) was sold for a hefty sum in 1988. The niche strategy once again had given birth to a major new category in which numerous powerful companies decide to play at the innovator's expense.

Tylenol, Pert Plus, Soft Soap, and Check-Up are just a few of the examples of superior product positioning of niche items giving birth to broad-based categories which help to revolution-ize the markets in which they compete. These are the principles utilized in conducting a marketing turnaround and they apply to businesses that are in trouble and are attempting to achieve their former glory as well as businesses that are niche players looking to expand their appeal to create dominant franchises.

14

TRADEMARK LEVERAGING

There are many instances in business where a company possesses intangible assets, including their brand names and trademarks, that are grossly underutilized vis-à-vis the real potential value they can create.

THE CONCEPT OF TRADEMARK LEVERAGING

Trademark leveraging can be defined as follows:

Taking an underutilized trademark and repositioning it to utilize the name to its full advantage or using the name to generate incremental volume and/or value that the name or trademark would not generate in its current form.

One of the first steps in trademark leveraging is gathering a list of all the brand names and trademarks, both active and inactive, that the firm owns and the categories those names are registered within. The company can then determine whether there are any trademarks that are not being used or are being underutilized and, if so, whether they can create new business using those assets. This "trademark leveraging" does not show up on a balance sheet, but if it did, unlike financial leverage or debt, which appears on the liability side of the balance sheet, it would most definitely appear on the asset side of the balance sheet.

Trademark leveraging is different than the concept of line-extension, in that line-extension simply takes a brand name and extends the product offering in a directly related sense, without materially changing the overall function or image of the parent brand. If a material change does occur, or the product enters a totally new area which may generate more volume than the original name itself generated, I would consider that trademark leveraging, not line-extension.

An important point to remember is that often the value of an intangible asset such as a trademark is never fully realized because the company which owns the name does not understand the true breadth of its appeal beyond its current use. For instance, when the Church & Dwight Company took the old-line Arm &

Hammer Baking Soda name and created Arm & Hammer Baking Soda Toothpaste, that was a classic example of trademark leveraging. Considering that many people use baking soda for anything from treatment of insect bites to cleaning the refrigerator, taking the name Arm & Hammer and positioning it as an efficacious dentrifice product was a bold move, but one that paid handsome rewards to Church & Dwight.

In other cases involving the concept of trademark leveraging, a small, seemingly insignificant brand name or descriptor is repositioned in a much stronger, more compelling approach. Rather than developing a totally new brand name, the company utilizes an existing name that has great potential beyond what it is registering presently (e.g., Power Stick Deodorant by Fabergé and Intimate Cologne by Revlon, discussed later in this section).

Alternatively, in the case of a product like Tylenol, which we discussed earlier, that is a classic example of line-extension: the firm took a 325 mg. analgesic and introduced a 500 mg. version of the product under the label "Extra-Strength." The extension is directly related to the primary function of the product and thus clearly extends the appeal of both the image and the function of the brand. Therein lies the difference between trademark leveraging and line-extension.

Most companies do not practice the art of trademark leveraging with the same degree of commitment as they practice line-extension, which is unfortunate given the huge potential for reward.

AN INTIMATE EXPERIENCE

A clear example of trademark leveraging is Revlon's Intimate Cologne. A best seller in the 1950s, Intimate by 1986 had a tiny franchise consisting largely of women over fifty. These women purchased their one bottle a year on special and the brand was all but forgotten at Revlon. Intimate was unable to attract younger users because of the decidedly dated character of the fragrance and its packaging.

While doing a lot of new product development work in the fragrance category, we at Revlon tested several names among consumers to see which ones would trigger a positive response. The name Intimate continually scored high among young women, who were unaware that there was a brand of that name on the market sold mostly to their grandmothers. Revlon was sitting on a very valuable trademark, which could be leveraged to the hilt in the sensual segment of the fragrance market. The prestige segment of this market was dominated by Yves Saint Laurent's Opium and Calvin Klein's Obsession. The strategic issues for Intimate were numerous:

1. How do you attract the youth market, which in this case was anyone under the age of fifty, to the brand Intimate?

2. How do you leverage the name Intimate to the teenage market, which clearly has shown a great tendency to purchase Obsession in department stores at very high prices on the one end of the spectrum, and purchases $50 million per year worth of musk products from a company called Jovan at $6.00 per bottle on the other end of the spectrum?

3. How can the name Intimate be used to create newness and excitement within the Revlon fragrance division and posture the line as a totally new concept from Revlon?

4. How do you minimize the risk of disenfranchising the existing user base of "old Intimate," or do you care that you lose the $2 million per year in annual sales which the brand does among women over fifty.

Revlon decided not to worry about losing the $2 million of existing franchise volume—we were willing to risk that to play the ball game at a higher level. We adopted the two-pronged strategy of going after the thirteen- to nineteen-year-old market with a new product introduction called Intimate Musk, a very youthful, sexy product that would appeal to the kids in that segment, with a very sophisticated package and fragrance. Second, we created a brand-new Intimate fragrance, which would be among the most provocative sold in the entire marketplace and would feature packaging and advertising that would truly characterize that positioning.

In a departure from conventional marketing tactics, Intimate Musk, which many would consider to be a line-extension product, was introduced in 1985 as the first entry from the new Intimate franchise and sold predominately in drug stores and mass retailers. The Intimate Musk fragrance was very well received by consumers. The packaging utilized a Matisse-like depiction of the bodies of a man and a woman intertwined, which became known as the Intimate symbol. This symbol, in red, orange, and yellow tones, was featured on a deep violet package—a very dramatic statement on the mass retail shelves. The Intimate Musk product launch occurred just ten months after the trademark leveraging process began and provided a totally new life to a tired old brand name.

We followed up the successful introduction of Intimate Musk with the launch of the new Intimate fragrance. At the top of the mass market category, with prices ranging from $10 to $20 a bottle, the Intimate fragrance paralleled the Vanderbilt product by Cosmair, and featured an upscale ivory package with gold piping around the edges and a smaller version of the new Intimate symbol.

The introductory advertising was created by Hill, Holliday Advertising and featured the highly controversial Intimate "ice cube" television ad. The ad was banned by several network censors from airing before 9 P.M. in some cases, and in other cases from airing at all, because it featured a very sensuous sequence of an ice cube running down the front of a woman's nude torso, guided by a man's finger. This juxtaposition of the man and woman was meant to be the embodiment of the symbol on the front of the package; it was truly provocative and considered a breakthrough in the market. The model used in that ad, Cindy Crawford, who was then a virtual unknown, became one of the hottest models in America and subsequently signed a very lucrative contract as the Revlon girl for its cosmetic line.

The combination of the Intimate ad and the furor surrounding its airing, the new fragrance and packaging for both Intimate and Intimate Musk, and Revlon's commitment to this tried and tested name in the category proved successful and generated incremental volume for the firm in excess of $15 million in the first year that they were both on the market, from a base of $2 million. Today, Revlon markets three Intimate products, the original "old Intimate product," Intimate Musk, and the new Intimate fragrance. The old Intimate product is referred to as Intimate Original, in somewhat the way Coca-Cola refers to its original product as Coca-Cola Classic.

15

REVLON FRAGRANCE DIVISION

Revlon's Fragrance Division was successful in other attempts at trademark leveraging as well. By June 1983, it was the largest popularly priced fragrance company in the world. Revlon fragrances included Charlie (the number-one brand in the market), Jontue (the number-two brand), Scoundrel, Intimate, Moon Drops, and Chaz For Men. The good news was that Revlon was number one overall in the market, with a market share of approximately 12 percent; the bad news was that the company had slipped badly from its lofty perch atop the market during 1982–83, and most of its brands were declining.

Charlie, the leader, was being attacked head-on by a new Warner Cosmetics fragrance called Vanderbilt (by Gloria Vanderbilt); Jontue was being very effectively assaulted by

Le Jardin de Max Factor, a brand that used Jane Seymour as its celebrity spokeswoman; Scoundrel was turning out to be an ill-conceived brand that had originally been destined to be named "Crawford" after the famous Joan Crawford, a plan that was scrapped after the infamous *Mommy Dearest* book was released.

Chaz For Men was an interesting case in that it never really was able to take off in the market for a whole host of reasons, not the least of which was that it was originally distributed only in department stores where it was sold at the women's Revlon counter. The brand was supposed to be the men's version of Charlie, both named after Revlon founder Charles Revson, but even with a then promising but relatively unknown male model named Tom Selleck (pre-Magnum P.I.), the brand was plagued with a variety of problems.

Revlon Fragrance was in a crisis mode and many of the techniques the firm had used so successfully during the 1970s and the beginning of the 1980s were no longer working in the marketplace. Revlon thus embarked on an aggressive program of attempting to repackage, reposition, and change the advertising and promotion on every single brand in the Fragrance Division at one time. In other words, the trademarks at Revlon needed to be leveraged while they still had some bearing in the market.

What the Fragrance Division needed was a classic marketing turnaround. Their loyal core group of users would be identified and protected, while the leverageable aspects of the various brands within the division would be identified and directed towards filling identified need gaps in the market. Given that Revlon was the number-one fragrance company in the market, the risks were obviously enormous, somewhat akin to "changing the course of a rocket in mid-flight." However it had to be done because share was eroding fast and in 1983 the Revlon Fragrance Division would lose approximately $6 million at the pretax level.

The marketing turnaround was launched by first creating specific mission statements for each of the brands and developing line positioning matrixes for each brand group (parent brand plus line-extensions). Next, elaborate market segmentation and need-gap analyses were performed, along with extensive brand image research to determine what consumers thought of Revlon's products. Last but not least, the Fragrance Division analyzed its production capabilities to determine how it could achieve unit volume efficiencies that would create favorable cost of goods.

This analysis allowed Revlon to create a host of new products and line-extensions for the fragrance division, designed to leverage the outstanding trademarks it owned and get products to market in an expeditious, economical fashion, with a minimal amount of financial risk. This would arrest franchise erosion on its mega brand assets.

In early 1984 the company introduced the fragrance market's first multiple scent line extension with the Fleurs de Jontue brand. Three fragrances—Iris de Fete, Rose de Mai, and Lotus de Nuit—featured the essence of the complex scent belonging to the parent floral brand, Jontue.

Market research indicated that Jontue users were intensely loyal to the floral scented subsegment of the fragrance market and that within their "wardrobe of fragrance" (the three to five brands each woman uses depending upon mood and occasion), they almost always gravitated towards other florals. This was unusual, because women who opted for the other segments of the fragrance market tended to look for variety within their fragrance wardrobes.

Accordingly, Revlon decided to create a true floral bouquet of fragrances, with the monochromatic scents of Iris, Lotus, and Rose used as alternatives to the complex bouquet that was Jontue. Fleurs de Jontue was an unqualified success, helping to increase Jontue volume by almost 40 percent and providing the aging brand with a much needed shot of vitality in the face of a tremendous competitive assault within the floral fragrance sub-segment.

In June 1985 Revlon made its move, introducing new packaging and graphics on Charlie, Jontue, Scoundrel, and Chaz. The retailer universe was notified well in advance and over six million empty boxes were sent out, called "redress" in the industry, to help retrofit the existing shelf stock and warehouse inventory of the retailers, in order to realize the volume and image impact of the move on a more immediate basis.

Revlon was alternately applauded, laughed at, and closely watched by both competitors and the retail community, who were looking for answers to these questions:

- Was the world's largest fragrance company just throwing its business away?
- Would the impact at point of sale help to stimulate more new users than it would disenfranchise existing users?
- Would current users and nonusers (wrongfully) perceive that what was in the bottle had also been changed (versus aesthetic changes only)?
- Did this move help more clearly define the positioning and intended occasion use for each of the non-cannibalistically positioned Revlon women's fragrances?

In addition to new packaging and new advertising, the company dramatically changed how the products were promoted to the consumer. The costly one-time-only special bottles that could not be moved into basic shelf stock when the promotional period was over were eliminated. Heretofore, these now-obsolete products had to be returned to Revlon, who had no way of profitably getting rid of the items. This strategy involving special one-time bottles and boxes had been further flawed, because a woman who received one of these fragrances as a gift and then went back to purchase the product for herself would be unfamiliar with the regular everyday packaging she saw at the store, which bore no resemblance to the gift packaging.

I call this deleveraging brand equity, which is a cardinal sin in the field of marketing. But Revlon was determined to make the consumer very aware of the new images for its fragrances and to further promote these products in an aggressive fashion at retail to achieve the following objectives:

- Create awareness, trial, and purchase of the Charlie, Jontue, Scoundrel, and Chaz brands at retail.
- Clearly delineate Charlie as a lifestyle brand, Jontue as a floral romantic brand, Scoundrel as a sensual brand, and Chaz as a strong masculine brand.

In order to drive the merchandise through at retail, Revlon devised an entirely new promotional system which promoted the basic packages of the various brands with a consumer overlay event (sweepstakes, mail-in offer, purchase with purchase, or gift with purchase) in a prepackaged countertop display unit. Not only did this help to market the brands in their primary, everyday packaging but it also achieved three critical objectives of any consumer packaged goods promotion:

- To realize the highly preferential cost-of-goods effect of utilizing basic, in-stock everyday product, rather than limited run specialty packs.
- To allow retailers to restock the promotional display when the prepacked product sells through because they have the same basic stock product on their existing display shelves.
- To make a consumer overlay premium (umbrella, cosmetic case, jewelry, tote bag, etc.) so desirable that con-

sumers will purchase the fragrance product just for the chance to acquire the premium (à la the Polo tote bags, Aramis umbrella, etc. in the prestige fragrance universe, where such items may be purchased immediately at the point of sale) through the mail.

Such items as a Chaz "undercover" umbrella, a Jontue "Lalique-look" floral stickpin, an offer for Scoundrel spokeswoman Joan Collins's autobiography *Past Imperfect,* and a Charlie lifestyle tote bag were part of the new promotional focus and the results were very successful.

Further, several new products and line-extensions from existing brand names were introduced in order to solidify those trademarks and create true power brands within the market that would be more effectively insulated from competitive assault. A major benefit of this strategy was that with minor graphic changes and different fragrances, almost all of the existing packaging (bottles, caps, etc.) and production components could be used, thus launching a new product with extremely desirable cost of goods. This in turn helped the cost of goods (due to volume component discounts) of the parent brands. Some of the new products introduced utilizing this strategy were as follows:

Charlie
- Charlie Naturals (trio of fragrances)
- Charlie Go-Lightly (bath and body line)

Jontue
- Fleurs de Jontue
- Jontue So-Softly (bath and body line)

Scoundrel
- Scoundrel Musk (teen-age fragrance)

Chaz
- Chaz Invigorating Body Spray

- Chaz Musk For Men

Intimate
- Intimate Musk
- New Intimate Cologne
- Intimate Original

The result of all these combined efforts from a very talented and committed marketing, sales, and product development organization was that the Revlon Fragrance Division underwent a total turnaround in profitability (to the tune of almost $10 million) in 1984 alone. The Divisional Fragrance market share as audited by A.C. Nielsen went from under 12 percent in March/April 1983 to over 16 percent in March/April 1985.

In addition, the Revlon fragrance franchise was expanded significantly within the younger age brackets because of the musk product introductions and the trio of fragrance brands. This obviously would have a very positive effect on the parent brand businesses at some point in the future when young users would logically ''graduate'' to the more sophisticated parent brand fragrances.

Perhaps the most fascinating of all the brand transformations within the Revlon Fragrance Division was the total reintroduction of the venerable Intimate brand, previously discussed in the last chapter. While there have certainly been more legendary marketing turnarounds than that of the Revlon Fragrance Division between 1983 and 1985, it is nevertheless one of the best examples of an attempt to turn around an entire company and all of its products in one fell swoop, in an industry where image is everything and life cycles are typically measured in months rather than years.

16

CREATING AND UTILIZING A MARKET SEGMENTATION ANALYSIS

An effective segmentation analysis can be one of the most valuable tools in the medicine bag of any marketing executive. Typically, new products that are introduced into the market and fail in a short time period can be traced to poor product positioning. In most cases, poor positioning is the result of an improperly conducted market segmentation analysis.

A comprehensive, focused, detailed segmentation analysis in a particular category will help the company highlight both consumer and retailer gaps in a specific market. Further, the market segmentation analysis will help the company determine what level of resources is required to penetrate that segment of the market effectively.

Unfortunately, many companies fail to conduct market segmentation analyses altogether, or they conduct rather cursory analyses and then enter a market blindly. In nine out of ten cases this scenario ends in a marketing disaster. The products introduced by these companies are typically referred to as "me too" products, which many companies introduce in the belief that any new competitor can achieve a reasonable share of a large market segment.

The supermarkets, drugstores, department stores, and specialty shops of the United States are currently littered with price-value products from small and large manufacturers that have no individual reason for being—they have no unique selling proposition, no unique packaging, and they are not the lowest priced entry in the category. Yet, despite all this, companies introduce these products under the presumption that if the market segment is large enough, consumers will gravitate toward a new entry for the sake of buying something new.

This is a completely erroneous assumption and one that helps to explain why nine out of ten new products fail within the first year on the market. Not only does the company suffer the embarrassment and financial loss of a new product failure, but its ability to enter new categories in the future may suffer. This is because those companies leave a negative impression on the retailer and a lack of confidence in that firm's ability to assess gaps in the marketplace.

When conducting a segmentation analysis the following key variables must be considered (see also Figure 6):

- Overall market size
- Individual product form variations (stick/roll-on)
- Price points
- Product sizes (small/user/economy)
- Gender splits (male/female)

- Age splits (adult/teen; 18–34/45–59)
- Functional splits (reduce pain/reduce fever)

The effective segmentation analysis will consider all of these variables that are pertinent and organize them into a format that provides a crystallization of the particular market under analysis. It is critical to understand all of the aforementioned variables and their respective impact upon the market, because improper segmentation of the target market may result in an erroneous estimation of volume potential for a particular new product.

For example, not segmenting the deodorant market by form or gender would lead to an overestimation of market size due to the inclusion of nonrelevant products. If the firm is introducing a new non-aerosol hair spray and the total hair spray market is considered to be the effective target universe, the company will be way off in its projections of market share because the non-aerosol segment is only 35 percent of the total category volume and women's hair spray accounts for 85 percent of the total non-aerosol segment volume.

Failure to recognize those points in the preparation of volume estimates for a new product introduction could lead to major

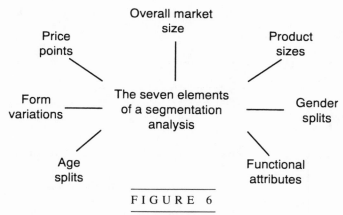

FIGURE 6

THE SEVEN ELEMENTS OF A SEGMENTATION ANALYSIS

problems for a firm in terms of profitability, inventory management, and tooling requirements. These reasons allow us to say that most new product failures result from improperly positioning a new product, the root of which usually lies in a less than thorough segmentation analysis.

The science of "niche marketing" is in effect a by-product of sophisticated market segmentation analysis, which helps to crystallize the competitive dynamics and purchase motivations of the market in total, often leading to the uncovering of "gaps" in the market. This is also referred to as "gap analysis," which used to be the domain of market research firms and has now crept into the skill-set of many marketing executives who have found progressive ways to uncover volume potential within seemingly overdeveloped markets.

SEGMENTING THE SHAMPOO MARKET

In the shampoo market, price is clearly the key determinant in the segmentation matrix. The four key pricing segments in that market from bottom to top are:

- Super-value ($.89–.99 retail)
- Price-value ($.99–1.89 retail)
- Mid-market ($1.89–2.98 retail)
- Up-market (over $2.99 retail)

In constructing a segmentation matrix for the shampoo market, the following key headings would be listed across the top of the matrix:

- Segment
- Retail pricing
- Major brands

- Percent of total market
- Key characteristics
- Current entries (from your firm)

Analyzing the shampoo/conditioner market as of the end of 1991, the matrix shown in Table 5 would apply. Where the company has no entries in particular segments, there is a "gap." Where entries in those segments were at one point stronger than they are today, there is "turnaround potential," and where entries in those segments are currently strong viable brands and effective contributors to the overall corporate volume mix, we say "hooray!" and look to the other segments within this category for future volume potential.

SEGMENTING THE DEODORANT/ANTIPERSPIRANT MARKET

In a category such as the deodorant and antiperspirant market the segmentation matrix would get much more detailed because this is a unique market that is not really driven by price sensitivity. The segmentation matrix for the deodorant and antiperspirant market would involve three key segments (see Table 6):

- Male brands
- Female brands
- Unisex or family brands

Next to each of those segments there would be form segments. For example, in the male brand segment there are sticks and there are aerosols. In the women's segment there are sticks, aerosols, and roll-ons. This is also the case in the family segment or unisex brand segment. The major brands are listed in each

TABLE 5

SHAMPOO/CONDITIONER MARKET SEGMENTATION MATRIX—1991

Segment	Pricing	Major brands	% Total	Characteristics
Up-Market	$2.98+	Pantene, Nexxus, Sebastian, Redken, Neutrogena, Jhirmack	10%	• Salon heritage • Broad assortment • Low advert./promo
Mid-Market	$1.89–2.98	Finesse, Sassoon, Silkience, Hälsa, Salon Selectives, Head & Shoulders, Pert Plus	40%	• Formula driven • Unique benefits • Heavily advertised • Moderate promos • Upscale packaging
Price-Value	$.99–1.89	Flex, Ivory, Suave, Condition, VO-5, Fabergé Organics, Aqua Net Silk Protein, White Rain	40%	• Large sizes • Lucrative deals • Heavy couponing • Cleanse/condition • Multiple SKUs • Heavy promotion • Modest ad levels
Super-Value	$.89+	St. Ives, UltraRich, AquaMarine, Unbranded	10%	• Large sizes • No advertising • Heavy trade deals • Low consumer promotion

TABLE 6

DEODORANT/ANTIPERSPIRANT MARKET SEGMENTATION—1991

Segment	Form	Major Brands	% Total Net	Key Characteristics
Male Brands	• Stick • Aerosol	Speed Stick, Old Spice, Right Guard, English Leather, Power Stick	30%	• Now dominated by sticks, aerosol rate of decline slowing • Odor protection is the number one attribute • Heavy advertising and consumer promotion (price) • Scent segmented
Female Brands	• Roll-on • Stick • Aerosol	Secret, Ban, Lady Speed Stick, Soft 'N' Dry Lady's Choice	35%	• Wetness protection is number one attribute • Historically dominated by roll-ons: sticks now growing • Heavy advertising and consumer promotion (price)
Unisex Brands	• Aerosol • Stick • Roll-on	Arrid, Sure, Dry Idea Mitchum, Dial, Degree	35%	• Aerosol form common to all (dual/all family usage) • Now expanding to all forms • Heavy advertising and consumer promotion (Price) • General deodorant/antiperspirant benefits

segment and within each form, along with the percentage of total market of each brand and each segment and the key characteristics found in each of those segments. As in the shampoo example, the company's own entries are listed in each of those segments to determine where leverage points are in an existing business and where the gaps lie that can be tapped on a near-term basis.

How to Use the Segmentation Analysis

For shampoos within the price-value segment (which does approximately 40% of category volume) for example, the following questions should be asked:

- Is our company a low-cost producer?
- Do we have the resources available from a marketing standpoint to effectively compete on a near-term basis?
- Do we have the sales organization to help get us the breadth of distribution required to compete in the price-value segment?

If the answer to all three of those questions is "yes," a company *might* consider entering a market segment that is very powerful—for example, one that possesses a 40 percent share of that market and does not appear to be in dire need of a "new brand."

If the answer to any of those three questions is "no," the company would be much better off looking elsewhere for near-term volume potential and attempting to find a segment of the shampoo market (or of another market) that can most effectively utilize its existing resource base, thus securing the highest return on investment.

SEGMENTATION: A WEAPON TO HELP WAGE THE "WAR IN THE STORE"

One of the biggest difficulties facing the retailer today in the United States is the proverbial "war in the store," whereby hundreds, if not thousands of manufacturers are assaulting the retailer with new products, line-extensions, repositionings, and the like. Because the space available within retail stores is not increasing, there is a huge attrition rate associated with the consumer products industry in this country. Retailers must constantly prune out brands that are not pulling their weight.

In addition, many manufacturers are forced to pay supermarket retailers "slotting allowances" (which are similar to entrance fees), in order to be allowed to play the game "the war in the store." Given the precious shelf space situation, retailers are becoming much more sophisticated in their marketing savvy and demand that manufacturers do effective segmentation studies prior to introducing new products. The retailer has to be convinced not only that the category the manufacturer is entering is viable, but that there is, in fact, a gap in that category from the retailer's perspective and that this new brand will help fill that gap.

In some cases, a retailer will shrink the number of brands carried in a specific category or market segment and stock only the market leaders, offering those products in a broader array of sizes and prices to help meet consumer demand. This strategy is based on the assumption that a few major brands will deliver greater sales volume over the long term than a cacophony of brands within a specific segment, with no one or two brands maintaining a dominant billboard presence on the shelf. This is why the U.S. packaged goods industry has become enamored with the concept of the line-extension in recent years.

If a company is lucky enough to possess a major brand, it will typically find it much easier to secure additional facings in retail outlets by line-extending that brand into a related (but incremental) segment of the market, rather than creating a totally new brand in a new segment. A common problem with this strategy is that often the segmentation analysis and positioning studies are not properly done and the manufacturer ends up introducing a line-extension with a high advertising/promotional cost and which inadvertently cannibalizes the parent brand. In this instance a line-extension is introduced off of a parent brand, which is costing the manufacturer more money to get into the store and to make the consumer aware of the product. Rather than adding to the total volume mix of the product line, it cannibalizes the parent brand often because of a poorly conducted segmentation analysis and line positioning matrix. The net effect of this move is that the company's overall position in that market becomes more vulnerable (if not weaker), and the profitability of the line declines.

Once an effective segmentation analysis has been done of the various market segments available to a firm, and the firm has decided to introduce a new product or a line-extension of an existing brand, the key question becomes "how do we do this?" How do we ensure that we have a comprehensive marketing program behind the new product or line-extension that will enable it to be effective in terms of generating market share and allow it to deliver satisfactory levels of profit and sales to the company?

17

THE NEW PRODUCT MARKETING DECISION TREE

The new product marketing decision tree (MDT) was something I created while at Revlon in 1985. The decision tree was later used to help engineer the turnarounds of Fabergé, Reebok, Revell/Monogram, Inc., and Catalina Swimwear and was extremely helpful in the development of numerous new products and line-extensions including:

- Intimate Fragrance
- Intimate Musk Fragrance
- Scoundrel Musk Fragrance
- Chaz Musk Fragrance
- Charlie Naturals Fragrance

- Charlie Go-Lightly Fragrance
- Moon Drops "Anti-Aging" Lotion
- Power Stick Deodorant/Anti-Perspirant
- Extra-Strength Brut 33 Deodorant/Anti-Perspirant
- McGregor Cologne
- Cut Guard Shaving Cream
- Fabergé European Salon Formula Haircare
- "The Pump" Sneaker by Reebok
- Reebok Hexalite Cushioning System
- Reebok Visible Energy Return System
- Reebok Energaire Cushioning System
- Luminators Hobby Kits
- Cote d'Azur Swimwear

The MDT is a fifteen-step regimen that plots the key decision points confronting a marketing executive during the new-product (line-extension) development process. Because of its encompassing nature, the MDT can also be used to develop a restaging or repositioning of an existing brand.

The "4-Ps" (price, product, placement, and promotion) are known to every student of business in the United States. However, not everyone knows how to use these variables within the framework of a cohesive marketing plan and how then to incorporate these elements into a mix that includes advertising and packaging. The critical element in maximizing the 4-Ps is synergy, and that is noticeably absent from the marketing plans of many major consumer product companies and small businesses all around the world. But because most brands do not have the spending power of a Coca-Cola, Pepsi, Budweiser, or Chevrolet, the use of synergistic elements in the marketing mix can help to increase the penetration, awareness, and conviction of the brand message.

The MDT is designed to help create a synergistic marketing program behind a major new product idea. The process utilizes variables within the decision tree to help direct the development of the marketing plan; to ensure that the product is properly positioned, priced, packaged, advertised, promoted, and distributed; and to increase the chances for success in a world where nine out of ten new products fail.

Like the road map the American Automobile Association issues when asked for driving directions to a particular destination, the MDT highlights key check points between point A and point B to make it easier to follow the route. The MDT utilizes key decision variables as markings along the road to launching a new product or line-extension, thus helping to deliver a focused marketing plan that should dramatically increase the chance for *success*.

How Does the MDT Work?

The MDT begins with a definition of the target audience and identification of the competitive brands in the marketplace (see Figure 7). Then it assesses the degree of fit between the product positioning and the target audience. This is extremely important to determine early on, before a firm becomes enthralled with a concept that may not be positioned for maximum impact within the identified market segment (from the segmentation analysis).

Clearly a major part of this assessment is the determination of whether the brand positioning is preemptive in the presence of competitive brands. In the absence of established brands within the target segment, it is necessary to determine how much consumer education is required before a product can be accepted.

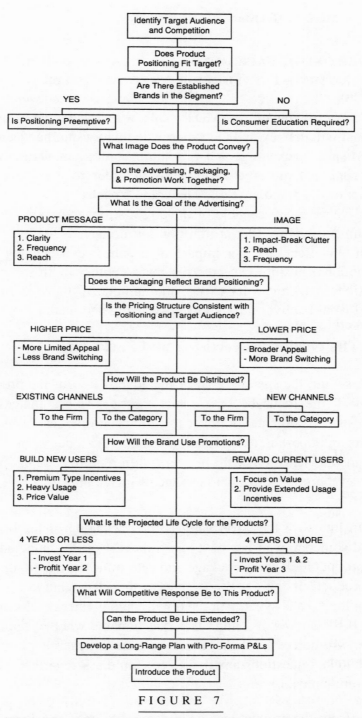

FIGURE 7

THE NEW PRODUCT MARKETING DECISION TREE

ADVERTISING, PACKAGING, AND PROMOTION—THE THREE-TIERED APPROACH

The next section of the MDT deals with the image that the product will convey and the synergistic relationship between the advertising, packaging, and promotional program. This three-part approach must be harmonious in order to maximize the impact of the brand at retail. The brand's packaging and promotional vehicles are capable of making a stronger impression on consumers in-store than a multimillion dollar advertising campaign. In effect, the net impact of a cohesive packaging and promotional posture can create a huge number of in-store impressions, which can far exceed the number of impressions the brand would deliver through its advertising and media program.

The Goal of Advertising and Packaging

What should the specific goal of the advertising for the product be? Will the focus be on product message (e.g., analgesics, toothpaste, detergents) or image (fragrance, cosmetics, fashion)? This is an important determination because the focus of the copy and media selection will be very different depending upon whether a product-attribute message or image objective is established.

In line with the advertising is the packaging of the brand. Could someone who has never seen the TV or magazine ad for that product look at the package and determine the positioning of the product? If the answer is "yes," then the relationship between the 4-Ps is synergistic, and will yield greater results in the end. If the answer is "no," it is questionable whether the consumer will derive any value from the communications program. The two key questions any marketer should ask regarding product communication are:

- Does the product lose its impact/message if consumers do not see the advertising?

• Does the packaging directly represent the image and spirit of the product positioning?

A "yes" answer to the first question and/or a "no" answer to the second question could spell serious trouble within the battlefield of the consumer product coliseum as you enter "the war in the store."

THE ROLE OF PRICING

The pricing structure must be consistent with the positioning of the product to effectively tap the target audience. The selection of a higher-price versus lower-price strategy will have a major influence on the breadth of appeal for a specific product. Further, the higher the price on a specific product, the less brand switching is likely to occur on a short-term basis, because the consumer is more committed to using the product. For this reason, the marketing strategies of luxury goods marketers must be decidedly different from those of commodity product marketers, where the pricing of the product has a direct impact upon the ability of a given company to attract new users.

SELECTING A DISTRIBUTION NETWORK

From a corporate standpoint, one of the critical determinants in a new product introduction is the selection of a distribution network. The first decision that must be made is whether the product will be distributed in existing channels or new channels. This determination must take into account both the company marketing the product and the category in which it will compete.

When firms start distributing to a new class of trade (e.g., to department stores when a firm is used to distributing in drug stores), they must compete with products already established in the distribution network within the target category. Conversely, a firm may distribute its existing products within a given class of trade, but will be a pioneer in the particular category it is entering with the new product. The assessment of capability is most important to the success of a new product or line-extension in that it can significantly affect a product's competitive position in the marketplace.

A classic example of the former was the very successful launch of Giorgio Perfume by Giorgio Beverly Hills in the early 1980s. The brand was the first perfume to use direct mail, magazine scent-strips to encourage purchase exclusively through the mail. After building significant volume and creating an aura of scarcity and exclusivity around the brand, Giorgio Beverly Hills was distributed into the upscale department store universe, breaking in at Bloomingdales in New York City. At that point, Giorgio management began utilizing a distributor because the retail store environment represented a new, untested environment for the product, although the trade channel was highly developed as an outlet for prestige fragrances from other firms.

A good example of the latter point is American Home Product's introduction of ibuprofen into the O-T-C market under the Advil brand name. Ibuprofen had been sold for many years under the brand name of Motrin as a prescription drug for pain relief. The image of the product was clearly enhanced by the fact that it had been available only through a doctor's prescription. When the FDA lifted the O-T-C ban on ibuprofen, American Home Products, through a distribution agreement with another pharmaceutical firm, began selling the brand Advil (ibuprofen) in drugstores across the United States.

There were several critical factors facing American Home Products as the O-T-C pioneer in the ibuprofen category, such as the daunting task of how to make people aware of the availability of Advil, the fact that it was previously sold only with a prescription, and how to achieve that without completely cannibal-

izing their existing portfolio of analgesics (O-T-C), including
Anacin (aspirin) and Anacin-3 (acetaminophen). The firm was
ultimately successful in marketing Advil brand ibuprofen and
was eventually followed into the O-T-C market by Bristol-
Myers' Nuprin, McNeil Consumer Product's Medipren, and Up-
john's O-T-C version of Motrin called Motrin IB.

THE PURPOSE OF PROMOTION

After the advertising, packaging, pricing, and distribution have
been aligned, the next key element of the marketing mix that
must be addressed is promotion. One important question is: "Is
the company's long-term goal (post-introduction) to build new
users or reward current users?" Many companies attempt to do
both at the same time and end up with ineffective promotional
programs.

The promotional techniques utilized in the two situations are
radically different and must be singularly focused to deliver powerful results. The decision in promotion is not unlike the media
decisions companies must make. The company can adopt a "dollars to sales" approach, which rewards current users, or it can
decide upon a "dollars to opportunity" approach, which helps to
build new users. The approach that the company ultimately se-
lects should be dependent upon whether the intent is to expand
the line via breadth or depth of usage.

THE PRODUCT LIFE CYCLE

A major element in the development of a new product is the projected length of its life cycle. Clearly, a product with a life cycle that is short (four years or less) will adopt a very different investment payout posture from those with projected life cycles of four years or more.

Companies that choose to compete in categories which require a high degree of consumer education will permit a competitor to invest in the category as a pioneer, knowing full well that the life cycle of the product will be four years or more. In this instance, the competitor may spend heavily in its brand's first year in order to capture initial users, but must then curtail the heavy level of investment in order to deliver a profit to the corporation.

The second company will enter the market after consumers have been educated about the product and will spend heavily on advertising and promotion, while the pioneers cut back. The second company thus capitalizes upon the heightened awareness of the category in general and moves consumers to its line-extension or new product with a perceived product advantage.

ASSESSING COMPETITIVE REACTION

One of the most important elements in the new product or line-extension development process in any business is the ability of the people in the company to assess the competitive response (reaction) to the introduction of the product, the opening of a new store (in the case of a retailer), or whatever. This will have a significant impact upon the nature and level of promotional activity associated with launching the product.

Part of this analysis is the assessment of line-extension potential for a new brand in order to increase overall awareness and penetration in the longer term. This certainly can help to insulate a product against direct assault in year two, by creating product news from the established brand name. In the field of consumer marketing this is called "the anniversary method."

By line-extending a product after a successful introduction, the firm obtains the ability to increase overall volume in the following ways:

- The pipeline effect of filling the retailers' shelves and warehouses with inventory of the line-extension, usually amounting to one-third of the anticipated first-year line-extension volume level.

- The ability to give existing users of the parent brand a newsworthy variant that can either be used in addition to the parent brand or provide an alternative to the new competitive entries in the market designed to attack your parent brand.

- Creating a preemptive strike in the category off of a now established power base in order to "eat up" shelf space in the category and help minimize or prevent competitive entries.

THE LONG-RANGE PLAN

In any new product or line-extension introduction, a long-range plan must be developed to determine the realistic life of the product. This is closely related to the life-cycle analysis presented and discussed earlier in this chapter. At minimum, a three-year pro-forma profit-and-loss statement is needed to assess the viability of a new product introduction. The P&L must be constructed in a most realistic sense in order to determine the proper level of investment in years one, two, and three of the product's life.

If the product is projected to have a very short useful life, year one will obviously be overloaded in terms of expenditure. In years two and three, advertising will typically be reduced and there will be more of a promotional focus (both trade and consumer) if the brand is in a price-value segment.

If the brand is in a mid-market or up-market segment, you will see a noticeable cutback in promotional activity and a transfer of those dollars into the advertising and media section of the mix in years two and three. Such brands must spend heavily on image- and/or function-related advertising to provide consumers with a reason (justification) to purchase a more expensive product.

The marketing decision tree helps marketing executives and small business owners take a good look at new product and repositioning ideas and ensure that they are properly positioned, supported, and distributed for maximum volume potential. Following the steps listed in this tree can help establish a systematic approach to developing a new product and provide a system of checks and balances for monitoring the plan to introduce the product.

18

THE BUSINESS BUILDING OCTAGON

The marketing decision tree provides a useful step-by-step procedure for developing and introducing a new product or line extension at the marketing management level. From the perspective of a more senior executive (president, executive vice-president, general manager), a tool that I developed while running the Revlon Fragrance Division was the business building octagon (BBO). The division was faced with the daunting task of trying to coordinate the marketing efforts of ten different fragrance brands across twenty-eight different countries in Revlon's first attempt ever at coordinated global marketing of fragrances. It was for purposes of facilitating the analysis and operation of the business on a common ground that I created the business building octagon.

The BBO is a tool that can be used to create overall business building, develop a growth strategy, and reassess the existing business to determine if its potential is being fully realized. It serves as a strategic road map for top managers, much as the MDT was designed for middle managers (''macro'' versus ''micro'' viewpoints). At first blush, the eight elements of the BBO seem common to everyday business management. The secret is that unless they are practiced in unison (and they rarely are), the effects of even well-conceived plans will be minimized. Lack of a cohesive, well-planned product strategy is one of the critical failings of most multi-brand companies.

The BBO is a sequential process that helps to provide discipline to a management team as they attempt to coordinate the efforts of a group of middle managers. The BBO is classical marketing management at its simplest level, using all of the basic strategic and analytical tools to create a plan to grow a business.

The eight steps of the BBO are as follows (see also Figure 8):

- Define category segments
- Develop products to penetrate new segments
- Position products in a non-cannibalistic way
- Price products in line with target audience
- Create packaging design that reflects positioning
- Distribute products in optimal size/flavor mix
- Use promotions to build new users
- Merchandise and advertise to create consumer pull

A review of each of these steps will show why this can be such an effective tool for helping to create a cohesive multi-brand marketing program.

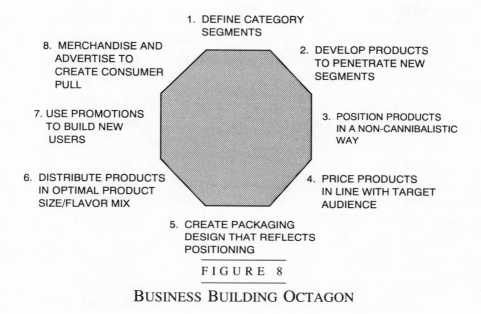

1. DEFINE CATEGORY
   SEGMENTS

8. MERCHANDISE AND
   ADVERTISE TO
   CREATE CONSUMER
   PULL

2. DEVELOP PRODUCTS
   TO PENETRATE NEW
   SEGMENTS

7. USE PROMOTIONS
   TO BUILD NEW
   USERS

3. POSITION PRODUCTS
   IN A NON-CANNIBALISTIC
   WAY

6. DISTRIBUTE PRODUCTS
   IN OPTIMAL PRODUCT
   SIZE/FLAVOR MIX

4. PRICE PRODUCTS
   IN LINE WITH TARGET
   AUDIENCE

5. CREATE PACKAGING
   DESIGN THAT REFLECTS
   POSITIONING

FIGURE 8

BUSINESS BUILDING OCTAGON

STEP 1: DEFINE CATEGORY SEGMENTS

Perhaps the most obvious step in the business building octagon deals with something that appears to be inherently self-evident: the definition of category segments within a particular market. One might wonder how a company could attempt to develop a business building plan for a particular product line without first understanding the dynamics and volume levels of the various sub-segments within the market, but this step is often either over-looked or performed in a cursory fashion. If you think back to Chapter 16 on market segmentation and the critical role it plays in the development of a unique product positioning and marketing strategy, you will understand the parallel between the lack of a sophisticated segmentation analysis and a cursory definition of market subsegments.

In defining category segments, the most obvious criteria to use involve the marketing positioning niches within the market.

For those who have never attempted to study the market in this manner, this step involves laying out all of the major brands within the market and creating a feature/benefit matrix detailing the specific attributes of the major brands.

Next, the analysis must cover the issue of whether the brands under evaluation compete within a specific segment or if they create segments unto themselves. For example, until 1988, the shaving cream market was composed of two key segments: gels and foams. While foams comprised 70 percent of category volume and gels possessed a 30 percent share, the gel segment consisted entirely of Edge Gel by S. C. Johnson, because that firm had an exclusive patent on the gel technology (until 1988).

Accordingly, prior to 1988, the analysis of the shaving market would have had to focus on the dynamics involved in the purchase decision and how to keep foam users from gravitating to gel products, rather than determining how to enter the fast growing gel segment due to the patent barrier. By crystallizing the purchase dynamics involved with the gel product, current and future makers of shaving foams could attempt to create specific niche strategies within the foam market that would also appeal to current users of gels.

In the fragrance market the definition of category segments is based upon attitudinal positionings, a rather ephemeral way to conduct market segmentation, but nevertheless the correct method for analyzing that market. The women's fragrance market comprises these category segments:

- Designer
- Sensual
- Romantic
- Lifestyle
- Musk

After the major brands in each of the segments is analyzed, the combined volume levels as a percentage of total category volume is listed on a pie chart or similar tool. In reviewing both the total number of players in each segment and the size of the segment, the marketing executive can make a preliminary decision about the wisdom of entering the market in general, and the segment in particular. Further, upon selecting the segments the firm intends to exploit, a complete analysis of the positionings of the incumbent products is essential to attempt to uncover a need gap or niche marketing strategy.

STEP 2: DEVELOP PRODUCTS TO PENETRATE NEW SEGMENTS

For a company with existing brands in a particular market, it is wise to adopt a strategy of developing products that penetrate new market segments, as highlighted in Step 1 of the business building octagon. Often the new segments of the market represent the most significant upside volume potential because they are fresh, different, and do not encroach on the existing stable of products in the company's portfolio.

In most cases, in order for a company to become a dominant player in a particular market and command the trade and consumer leverage that comes along with that distinction, it must have multi-segment product representation appealing to the broadest possible range of consumers. A good example of this is the soft-drink market, where the Coca-Cola Company, makers of the most famous consumer product of all time, have adopted a multi-segment strategy in an attempt to achieve market leadership. In addition to Coca-Cola and the various line-extensions off of that brand (e.g., Caffeine-Free, Cherry Coca-Cola), the firm also markets a variety of soft-drink products in the lemon-lime (Sprite), orange (Minute Maid), diet (Diet Coke), and fresh

(Fresca) segments. Each of these entries penetrated a new segment for the company and helped to expand the potential universe of users of Coca-Cola Company products.

This strategy of diversifying a company's product portfolio also helps to lessen risk, in that it serves to insulate the firm against taste, image, functional, and fashion trend shifts, which can significantly reduce market presence in a very short period of time (e.g., the wine cooler market, which grew very quickly and then after a huge competitive war, the market virtually dried up in a very short time frame).

The Corporate Capabilities Matrix (see Chapter 10), which dealt with the various production capacities within a specific company and how to use untapped capacity to drive a new products program, can be effectively utilized within Step 2 of the Business Building Octagon. Specifically, if new segments within a category have already been defined, the CCM can indicate whether they can be penetrated quickly and at a lower cost level.

Alternatively, if new segments of the market have not been defined, assessment of the capability of the manufacturing facility can lead to the development of a new segment that is production or technologically based (e.g., development of a hair mousse product within the styling product segment by manufacturers of aerosol products).

STEP 3: POSITION PRODUCTS IN A NON-CANNIBALISTIC WAY

The concept of product positioning is perhaps the most critical element in the determination of market success, and from the perspective of running an entire company, the effective positioning of the stable of products so that they do not "cannibalize" one another is as important a task as senior management will face.

Many firms end up introducing new products and/or line-extensions that are aimed (intentionally or unintentionally) directly at an existing product within the firm's portfolio. Frequently the new product carries a hefty advertising and promotional budget, innovative packaging, and new and different merchandising at the point of sale. Further, as is the case with most new products, a trade allowance program which offers the retailer lucrative discounts is typically a major element of the new product marketing program, making it much easier to attract new, bargain-conscious customers during the early stages of the product's life.

The problem with such new product strategies is that if the product happens to be launched into the same segment as one of the firm's existing (mature) brands, the new product has a double-negative effect:

- It creates an image of forced obsolescence for the existing category entry.
- The firm is spending heavy amounts of money to attract the very users it already has purchasing one of its existing brands at higher margin levels.

Often this is the result of the internal competitiveness within major corporations, whereby separate groups within the company are in direct competition with each other. Further, where the groups may report to different individuals, the overall strategic encroachment of one brand upon another is often not highlighted until very late in the new product development process, when the president or vice-president of the company eventually uncovers the potential problem. At that point it is often too late to change the strategy due to heavy expenditures of dollars that have already been invested in the project, and the product goes to market as planned.

Such problems can best be addressed in two ways, neither of which is mutually exclusive:

- Organize the company into functional groups by market segment in order to maintain continuity of thinking and avoid direct competitive conflict with a viable existing asset.
- Utilize the mission statement and line positioning matrix vehicles described in Chapter 8 to help highlight the products within the company and where the potential for cannibalization appears greatest.

From a financial standpoint, the effective execution of Step 3 of the BBO will help the company significantly increase its upside profit potential as a total entity and help to enhance the positive financial effects of possessing "cash cows" within a stable of products.

STEP 4: PRICE PRODUCTS IN LINE WITH TARGET GROUPS

A major mistake that is made by many companies, large and small, is the way in which they determine pricing of a particular product. Unfortunately, utilizing the cost-plus pricing method may result in a price that yields terrific gross margin, but may knock the product out of the competitive arena required to generate significant volume.

Therefore, the firm may have a product that appears to be very profitable on a per unit basis, but because of the improper price point the product will never realize its full volume potential, and the absolute level of penny-profit it can deliver to the company will be significantly less than it could have been.

The concept of pricing a product to achieve maximum dollar (or penny) profit is in many cases diametrically opposed to the concept of gross margin preservation. When utilizing the penny-profit approach to pricing, the company determines where the product would be most advantageously priced from a competitive standpoint and where the most volume can be generated. Thus, the firm may be sacrificing gross margin on a per unit basis, but because it will sell many more units at the lower price, the overall level of profit dollars that become available to help cover overhead and other costs could be significantly greater in the aggregate.

When pricing a product, whether via the cost-plus or the market-driven method, the major variable that must always be of the utmost importance is what the target audience expects to pay. This is an issue that often is not researched by the company marketing the product, and this can undermine even the most innovative marketing program. It is a shame to see outstanding products marketed by companies at the wrong price level. When these products fail to realize the level of volume that was originally projected, they are removed from the market. Occasionally, they are purchased by other companies, who have better overall cost structures, enabling the product to be marketed at a lower price, or who have the insight and support data to create a pricing level that will increase consumer demand.

STEP 5: CREATE PACKAGING DESIGN THAT REFLECTS POSITIONING

In line with the concept of synergistic marketing outlined earlier in this book in the Marketing Decision Tree section, creating a package for a product that accurately reflects the positioning of the product is a critical element of the marketing/communications mix. Advertising is an effective way to build awareness for a product, but many more impressions are created at the point of sale and communicated via the outer packaging of the product.

Often the packaging of a product bears no relation to the positioning communicated through the advertising, merchandising, and promotional campaigns, creating a distorted message to the consumer at the most critical venue: the retail shelf. The power of packaging in the field of consumer products is largely underutilized as a marketing tool, especially given the predominance of impulse purchases in the marketplace.

In order to effect brand switching from a competitor's product, the company must design the packaging to clearly communicate everything that is deemed critical to the purchase decision. The primary elements should be communicated via the brand name, the coloration and design elements, and the like, whereas the secondary imagery and the functional attributes should be communicated via the body copy on the front and back of the package.

The Revlon Fragrance Division, discussed earlier in this book, possessed the quintessential lifestyle brand in Charlie, the classic romantic fragrance in Jontue, the ultimate provocative, sexy fragrance in Scoundrel, and a masculine, outgoing fragrance in Chaz. But while the advertising and marketing programs certainly reinforced the imagery of those products, the packaging clearly misrepresented the positionings of what are the consummate image products (fragrances).

The Charlie fragrance was packaged in powder blue with subtle zodiac symbols screened and embossed all over the package. The impression was of a sedate, feminine, lightly scented product—in fact, the antithesis to the energetic, bold image of the Charlie woman. During the Fragrance Division's turnaround effort, the color of the redesigned Charlie package was changed to an electric blue and the logo was given a more contemporary look reminiscent of the signature of the famous sculptor Alexander Calder. Thus the image created by the advertising and promotion was now embodied in the packaging, and created a synergistic, cohesive message to the consumer.

The classic, romantic Jontue fragrance was reflected in its compelling TV ads, which depicted a woman in a sheer chiffon dress riding bareback through a field adjacent to a French country estate, to the sound of the distinctive Jontue bugle call. The promotions on the brand also used floral, romantic imagery, with such purchase-with-purchase premium items as a crystal floral stickpin, a gift certificate for flowers through Teleflora, and a parasol/umbrella with a floral print pattern. All of this helped to create a unique and compelling image for the brand, but since it was considered unthinkable in the fragrance business to show the outer package in advertising (the perfume bottle itself was always shown), the consumer did not know what the box looked like on the retail shelf.

Unfortunately, what they saw was a plain white box with a blue script Jontue logo screened discreetly across the front panel. Hardly what one would expect from the quintessential floral, romantic fragrance. Moreover, in early 1984, Jontue faced a direct frontal assault from Le Jardin de Max Factor, utilizing Jane Seymour as its spokesperson and featuring a Monet-like floral package. Given the consumer confusion that goes on at retail, and the fact that many men who purchase fragrances as gifts for women have only hazy recollections of the ads they see prior to Mother's Day or Christmas, Jontue's lack of a floral, romantic package was virtually swaying the purchase tide over to the competition.

To bring the packaging in line with the fragrance's image, a peach colored package with an airbrushed effect was created, with a beautiful white flower embossed on the face of the package and the Jontue logo tucked underneath the petals of the flower. This package communicated everything that was said in the Jontue advertising, and Revlon's market research indicated that people were more likely to associate the advertising with this package than with the old one.

These two examples show how inefficient (not to mention confusing) it can be for a brand's imagery to be inconsistent with the rest of its marketing effort. Having a package that truly reflects the brand's positioning dramatically increases its potential for being selected by impulse shoppers, who may be unaware of the brand's marketing/advertising messages but who make on-the-spot purchase decisions based upon what they see in front of them on the retail shelf.

STEP 6: DISTRIBUTE PRODUCTS IN OPTIMAL SIZE/FLAVOR MIX

This step requires the establishment of discipline within the company's sales and marketing departments in an attempt to optimize the shelf space being allocated to its products by the retailer. Further, this step requires the integration of the manufacturing and warehousing functions with the marketing/sales area, in order to ensure that the mix of merchandise produced and warehoused is consistent with the retail distribution mix.

If this sounds like basic blocking and tackling, then why are manufacturers constantly dealing with the de-listing (elimination) of slow-moving items that tend to cast an undeserving pall over the balance of the line, which may be doing very well at retail. This is the "one bad apple" that can spoil the whole bunch, and can truly work against even the most dominant manufacturers in a particular market segment.

Think of the situation at the retail store level. The square footage of the existing store does not change and the size of the shelving units is constant. Further, it is very unusual for a retailer to expand the linear footage devoted to a particular market or segment of the market. Therefore, as a barrage of new products and line-extensions hits every year, the retailer is faced with the never-ending process of pruning the existing retail assortment to accommodate some of the exciting, new, heavily supported entries that appear viable. In the retailing trade this is often referred to as an "SKU purge"—the elimination of slow-moving stock-keeping units. An SKU is any individual item that would be entitled to an individual facing on the retail shelf, including variants in size, flavor, scent, performance, and so on.

Given the fact that the retail shelf space issue ("the war in the store") never goes away, it is imperative that the manufacturer be able to supply the items that the consumer has indicated a strong willingness to purchase. A secondary issue related to retail distribution, and one no less important to the company, is the coordination of the manufacturing/warehousing process (the forecast) with the retail distribution pattern.

In firms with poor interdepartmental communication or ones that have aggressive inventory build programs, a potentially disastrous situation can arise: The warehouse may be full of products that are out of the current retail mix. Thus, working capital has been eaten up by these slow-moving items, which cannot be translated into full revenue dollars (they may have to be closed out) and which occupy precious space in the warehouse.

The ensuing "dump" which may have to take place can ruin a business and undo years of brand image building and retailer relationships based on preservation of profits via sales at full retail prices. Additionally, this situation provides the perfect opportunity for a competitor to approach the retailer in pursuit of precious shelf space and market leverage, and suggest the deletion of a product line in its entirety at worst, or at best suggest the paring back of the SKU assortment.

Therefore, the senior management team has to sit down and carefully plan for the anticipated consumer demand for each item within the product line. This plan must then be continually revised, taking into account any point-of-sale data available from the retailer to adjust the production forecast and manage the turn level of the retail inventory. Failure to do this can cause severe, possibly irrevocable damage to a brand, and can cause a precipitous drop in volume and effect a significant alteration in the retail mix.

STEP 7: USE PROMOTIONS TO BUILD NEW USERS

As discussed earlier in Chapter 18 about the marketing decision tree (MDT), promotional campaigns can be used either to attract new users to the brand or to reward existing users. For purposes of the proactive use of the BBO and to be true to the spirit with which it was created, this section will focus on the use of promotions to attract and build new users.

Depending upon what market the product or company is competing in, the use of promotions can be a very effective vehicle for producing instantaneous increases in sales volume by attracting new users or brand switchers to the product. The goal of advertising is to create an image and communicate the attributes of the product; the role of merchandising is to preemptively display the product for maximum visibility; the role of promotion in a business building mode is to attract new users to the brand.

There are several techniques and schools of thought on how best to attract new users to a brand and to accomplish the even more difficult task of encouraging users of a competitive product to switch brands. Suffice it to say there is no one right way to execute a promotional plan, but there are some general criteria that should be followed when operating within a business-building (rather than a defensive) mode. The following techniques are designed not to attract new users, but be more appropriate for rewarding existing users:

- Low-value, cents-off coupons (less than 10 percent off)
- Bonus packs/economy sizes (free ounces)
- Mail-in premium offers
- Frequent purchaser programs

These techniques are not recommended for attracting new users, because if consumers are unsure about buying a brand, offering a small discount, or more of the product for the same price, or a premium that requires the purchase of that product—much less encouraging them to purchase that product many times to accumulate purchase credits—will not be enough to cause them to switch from their existing brand or enter the market for the very first time.

Rather, the techniques that should be employed to attract and build a new user base for the product should focus on highly desirable, instant gratification methods that in and of themselves diminish or virtually eliminate any perceived purchase risk to the consumer. Specific examples of promotional techniques that will help to generate new users include the following:

- Free purchase rebate
- High-value introductory coupon (making regular size priced like a trial-size)
- Instant gratification gift-with-purchase
- High-value trade-in credit

Obviously, if there were a surefire method to generate new users everyone would use that technique all of the time. However, these vehicles are time-tested and have proven to be the most effective means of generating new users, assuming that the product, packaging, pricing, and advertising are all sufficiently strong enough to do the things they are supposed to do. If they are, the use of aggressive promotional vehicles can help to generate a high level of new trial—whether or not those new triers become regular users depends very heavily on the efficacy and imagery of the product.

Let us review the four aforementioned promotional techniques designed to attract new users:

- *Free Purchase Rebate.* A rebate is used to attempt to remove all monetary risk associated with the initial purchase of the product. In effect, this technique creates strong initial consumer demand for a new product and establishes a credibility base with the retailer, while giving consumers the chance to "purchase" the product at retail with no risk. Since more than half of the purchasers will never send in the proof-of-purchase to receive their full refund, this technique is much more financially sound than mailing out free samples to people or offering the product free at the point of sale with a coupon.

• *High Value Introductory Coupon.* This is an effective vehicle to drive initial consumption because it allows the manufacturer to sell a regular-sized product post-coupon for a trial-sized price. Many times a newspaper ad for a food or drug store will offer the product at $1.49, say, less manufacturer's coupon of $1.00 (67% off), bringing "your cost" to just $.49. That will almost certainly gain the product's manufacturer prominent end-aisle placement in the store and primary mention in the retailer's advertising vehicle.

• *Instant Gratification Gift-with-Purchase:* This technique is often used in image businesses such as cosmetics, fragrances, and athletic footwear, where it is very difficult to sell a "functional" benefit. The instant gift with purchase helps to set the tone for the product and provides yet another incentive to purchase the product. By enticing the consumer to purchase because a high-perceived value premium item, although this is the ultimate form of borrowed interest marketing, in actuality it is just another vehicle being employed to help establish the image of the product. This technique is often used by magazines to motivate people to buy annual subscriptions at major reductions off the cover price and still receive a highly valued premium item that ideally is thematically linked to the positioning of the magazine (e.g., *Sports Illustrated*'s sports watch, *National Geographic*'s world atlas, *Barrons'* financial calculator). Instant gratification is the name of the game when trying to attract new users to a relatively high-priced product, where the risk of mistake is perceived to be high and thus a value rationale must be employed.

• *High-Value Trade-In Credit*. When trying to get users of a competitive product, who are probably very happy with it to switch to your product, you must attempt to take them out of their normal purchase cycle and consider your product in an unencumbered mental environment. Specifically, that means that, if I own a pair of Reebok athletic shoes and you want me to try a new shoe from L.A. Gear, you must attempt to give me a reason to get rid of my Reeboks before I had planned to and reduce my risk of mistake with the new purchase. An excellent way to do that is to offer a trade-in credit from the competitor's product against a purchase of your product. In this example, offering a $20.00 trade-in credit on the Reeboks against the purchase of the new L.A. Gear shoes is a way of making me buy a new pair of shoes before I may have been ready to, and my perceived risk has been lowered significantly by the $20.00 trade-in credit. This technique is often employed in industries where the purchase cycle is relatively long (once every six months or more) such as stereo equipment, large appliances, athletic footwear, and watches. By penetrating the consumers' psyches even before they have entered the purchaser mode, sometimes traditional brand allegiances can be effectively broken. In such instances the purchase is often the result of "want," not "need," which brings with it an entirely different set of motivating elements.

An entire book could be devoted to the concept of using promotions to generate new users for a product line, but the techniques discussed here in Step 7 of the Business Building Octagon are the most effective methods available today and have been used with a very high rate of success.

STEP 8: MERCHANDISE AND ADVERTISE TO CREATE PULL-THROUGH

There is no one proper way to merchandise and advertise a brand or company, given the very different types of communications tasks individual companies face in their respective markets. However, the use of a cohesive, synergistic marketing communications strategy, or what I call "power marketing," can help to overcome budgetary inadequacies when competing against larger, better capitalized foes. In such cases, the "power marketing" approach can distance the brand from the competition and force the rest of the field into adopting niche strategies—"fighting over the crumbs."

The previous seven steps of the BBO have outlined a methodical, systematic way to define the market; identify the emerging growth segments; position the product so that it does not cannibalize the products the firm already owns; price the product in line with the target audience's expectations; package and position the product to exemplify the brand; carefully select the proper number and variety of SKUs to distribute into the retail universe; and devise a promotional campaign to attract new users to the product line.

All that is left is the creation of the strategy that will ultimately pull the product through at the retail level, and that is the job of the advertising and merchandising in conjunction with the promotional campaign. The broadcast/print strategy for the product should be in line with the steps outlined in the Marketing Decision Tree, depending upon whether imagery or function is the primary marketing platform. If the product is image driven, the goal of the advertising is three-pronged:

- Impact—break through the clutter
- Reach
- Frequency

In the case of an image-driven product, the key element is making the greatest number of people notice the advertising right away, without having to see several exposures before the product image registers. The introduction of Obsession Cologne by Calvin Klein in the late 1980s was an example of this strategy, which employed bizarre, highly controversial ads both on television and in magazines to create a media event unto itself.

For Obsession, the goal was certainly to reach as many people as possible quickly with a clutter-breaking ad that would create a unique, compelling, and—it was hoped—motivating message. That technique has proven very effective over time, but definitely requires a level of creative brilliance that is hard to come by.

In the case of a product employing a functionally driven message strategy, the key elements of the advertising/media strategy must be the following:

- Clarity of message
- Frequency
- Reach

A good example of this would be an analgesic product like Tylenol or Advil, both of which rely on the message of efficacy and safety to generate purchase intent. For them, no amount of imagery can compensate for a lack of those two elements in the communications process. The message must be "You can't buy a more potent pain-reliever without a prescription" (Extra-Strength Tylenol) and "Hospital-safe, doctor recommended." This clarity of message is essential for a product of that nature.

From a media standpoint, the goal is first to hammer home that point often enough so that it registers, using a frequency media strategy, and trying to reach as many people as possible. On an efficacy-based message, focus and intensity are of greater importance than occasional presence to large masses of people. Before Tylenol was ever advertised on television, the manufacturer utilized an extensive doctor, pharmacist, and hospital staff "detailing" program, whereby representatives of the company would call on those individuals and extoll the virtues of the product, leaving free samples and patient benefit literature. While the build with this type of strategy is undoubtedly slower than the quick-strike potential of the image "clutter-buster" attack, the long-term benefits of a loyal franchise are far greater.

The same can be said of the merchandising aspect of a marketing program, where many of the same elements employed in the advertising medium must be applied in a synergistic manner to the in-store merchandising program. In the case of image-driven products, that means utilizing the same photographic images on display units as are featured in the ads. In merchandising functionally driven products, the point-of-sale approach is almost always educationally based, with a concentrated focus on communicating the key attributes included in the advertising message, but perhaps stated in a more elaborate manner.

The concept of driving a business at retail via the use of advertising and merchandising depends on the quality of the creative product and the degree to which it carries the same message and imagery as the balance of the marketing mix elements. Suffice it to say that in the absence of great creative product, continuity of marketing message—from positioning to pricing to packaging to promotion to advertising/merchandising—can overcome the lack of uniqueness in the creative message, can make the marketing of the product infinitely more successful, and will build much higher awareness in the minds of the consumers.

19

BUSINESS OUTLOOK FOR THE 1990S

The magic buzzwords in the 1980s were "leveraged buyouts (LBOs)" and "junk bonds." The buzzwords for the 1990s will turn out to be "turnaround" "restructure," and "prepackaged bankruptcy." It is ironic (but true) that there is a distinct cause-and-effect relationship between the buzzwords of the 1980s and those of the 1990s. The turnarounds, restructurings, and prepackaged bankruptcies that have already started to appear in great numbers early in the decade are in large part due to the overzealous predictions of those who originally did the LBOs, combined with a major shift in the overall business climate in the United States.

In the 1980s, low-money down and a big burden of debt could buy you a major corporation, regardless of whether or not you or your firm had the reputation, capital, and know-how to manage the acquired company effectively. The assets of the company to be acquired were pledged as collateral and often sold off ("busted up") to pay down the heavy debt load, leaving a significantly scaled-down version of the acquired firm. The projections of 20 to 30 percent growth that often accompanied the LBO transactions many times did not even come close to reality and many solid, viable companies, with healthy operations and good operating income levels (EBIT—earnings before interest and taxes) were forced into Chapter 11 because the debt service they carried was in excess of the actual (versus projected) earnings they generated.

The standard joke was, "The good news is we made $50 million of operating income this year, up from $40 million last year, the only problem is that our debt payments amount to $65 million." The end of that story is, "And oh! by the way, here are the keys to the front door."

In the 1990s, several of these LBOs will undergo restructurings or prepackaged bankruptcies, which in effect make them prime candidates for turnaround teams. The restructuring involves going to the debt holders of the LBO and offering them an equity swap in return for the debt (bonds, bank debt) they hold, in order to unencumber the highly leveraged company and give the debt holders the potential to realize significant value appreciation as owners of the company. This is often done in cases where the company, the LBO owners, and the debt holders realize that the chance of the firm paying the interest required on the debt instruments they hold is suspect, and furthermore would constrain the company to the point where a reoccurrence of the situation would have to be dealt with in the near future without some debt relief.

The case of the prepackaged bankruptcy is very similar to the classic restructuring described above, except that the company has been judged to be virtually insolvent. There is no chance it can make its current interest payments and there is the very real likelihood that the firm will go into the arduous proceedings associated with a Chapter 11 bankruptcy filing in the very near future. In such cases, the company and its owners approach the bondholders and their creditor committee and present the terms of a bankruptcy settlement, involving a debt-for-equity swap and a restructuring of the ownership, bank covenants, and so on. This saves the time, expense, and anguish involved when a court-appointed administrator or judge presides over the financial affairs of a company, often crippling the firm and making the flow of dollars much more difficult.

In effect, a prepackaged bankruptcy is just that, the company and the debt holders go to the judge and state that they have already worked out a mutually agreeable settlement and the judge usually rules in favor of the agreement. By avoiding the court administration procedures the company has a better chance of focusing on the operation of the business, rather than on the management of the Chapter 11 process. Prepackaged bankruptcies have become much more prevalent in the 1990s and look like the wave of the future for the overleveraged transactions of the previous decade.

So where does that leave us from a business perspective? It brings us to the very thrust and focus of this book: *The Turnaround Prescription*. After the companies have been scaled down, restructured, or moved into prepackaged bankruptcy, the only way for anyone to make any money on the newly acquired equity in the company is by performing a "turnaround." It is my belief—having been through quite a few of these situations and using the "prescription" outlined in this book, along with the analytical techniques to help create the growth strategies for the entities—that *The Turnaround Prescription* will serve as a handbook for the 1990s. While we cannot teach anyone how to create the big idea, we can certainly provide the framework for uncovering the key problems in a business and how to go about setting the firm back on the right track. The rest is up to you, the manager, to determine how best to put these principles to work within your company and realize the benefits they can provide.

It is my belief that the 1990s will be an acquisition-oriented decade which, while not on the scale of the 1980s, will feature better structured deals with a greater chance for ultimate success. The focus will be on the creation of value beyond that which the existing entity has been able to realize, and financial institutions will require more realistic debt-to-equity ratios, while demanding an equity participation in addition to the interest on the debt.

The 1990s will be the decade of the "value merchant" or "business builder," as opposed to growth by pure acquisition. The capital structures of many firms will be such that the multiplier effect of achieving real base business growth will provide impressive increases in profitability and shareholder value. With the fear of an imminent hostile takeover greatly diminished compared to the heyday of the "raider parade" in the 1980s, U.S. companies will have the opportunity to focus on the long-term aspects of their businesses and attempt to solidify the foundations of the core business, while planning for real growth through internal development and expansion. This will help to increase the competitive posture of U.S. manufacturing firms, which suffered so dearly in the global market during the previous decade, as the overburdened debt situation prevented many companies from being able to fund necessary capital improvement required to maintain a dominant manufacturing/technological advantage.

More and more deals in the 1990s will feature the infusion of real capital in exchange for equity stakes in the companies, thus reducing the need for external bank financing and the associated interest burden. For those investors and companies who are liquid, the investment opportunities will seem endless. For those with the ability to infuse both financial and human (know-how) capital, the 1990s should truly be an investor's panacea, where the benefits realized will be rooted in a more solid foundation and the long-term value of the acquired/turnaround property will be more significant than it has been in recent memory.

To all who have read this book purely from an informational standpoint, I hope you found it interesting and in some way meaningful to your vocational experience. To those who purchased the book because of a direct need in the area of turnarounds or increasing the value of a troubled concern, I hope that by following some of the principles in this book you will realize the growth in sales and profitability required to make your company a success.

Lastly, to those in academia who are students of business at the undergraduate or graduate level, I hope that *The Turnaround Prescription* provided you with an understanding of how a real-world business dilemma can be uncovered and ultimately solved through the use of a methodical, analytical blueprint that does not require the intellect of a brain surgeon nor the patience of a saint, neither of which I have ever been accused of possessing.

As the old saying goes, "If you don't know where you're going, any road will take you there." *The Turnaround Prescription* should definitely help you to figure out where you are going and how to get there. Whether you ultimately reach that destination is entirely up to you.

INDEX